AURA GARDEN GUIDES

Elisabeth Manke

Houseplants

AURA BOOKS

Aura Garden Guides

Houseplants
Elisabeth Manke

Original German language edition:
Gärten leicht und richtig
Der Zimmerpflanzenpflege
© 1993 BLV Verlagsgesellschaft
mbH, München, Germany

This edition produced by:
Transedition Limited for
Aura Books, Bicester
and first published in 2002

English language edition
© 1995 Advanced Marketing (UK) Ltd.,
Bicester, England

English language translation by:
Andrew Shackleton for Translate-A-Book,
a division of Transedition Ltd.,
Oxford

Typesetting by:
Organ Graphic, Abingdon

10 9 8 7 6 5 4 3 2 1
Printed in Dubai

ISBN 1 901683 84 2

Photographic credits
Apel 25, 30 top, 31, 65; Eisenbeiss 46, 49
right, 51, 75, 92; Groebe 49 left, 81;
Henseler 26, 27 top left; Manke 10, 12/13,
14, 15, 28, 37, 38; Morell 34/35, 47 top,
56, 76/77, 78, 88/89; Niehoff 9, 23, 40,
93, 95; Redeleit 4/5, 41, 87; Reinhard
84/85; Sammer 8, 16, 19, 21, 22, 24,
45/46, 55, 72 left, 77, 83, 89, 90, 94
backcover left; Seidl 10/11, 27 (except
top left), 47 bottom, 64, 67, 69, 82/83,
frontcover; Stein 8 bottom right, 17, 29,
32, 33, 79, backcover right; Strauss 2/3,
6/7, 7, 20, 30 bottom, 35, 36, 39, 42,
42/43, 43, 44, 45, 48, 50, 52/53, 53, 54,
57, 59, 60, 61, 62, 63, 66, 68, 70, 70/71,
72 right, 73, 80, 86, 91

CONTENTS

Living with plants

'Plants are just like obstinate people: they will do anything for you if you handle them properly...' So said Goethe — one of the world's greatest poets.

Houseplants need plenty of care and attention, not to mention a great deal of effort. You can't just treat them as part of the furniture. If you don't look after them, you will never have the pleasure of seeing them grow and flourish over the years. If you can, you should do something to them every day — watching them, caring for them and actively helping them to develop. This is what makes houseplants so delightful to work with: this small domestic nature reserve will offer new challenges every day.

Besides general care, houseplants also benefit from being carefully arranged. If anything, though, too little planning is better than too much. All plants should harmonise with their surroundings. A spacious, high-ceilinged room is the ideal place for large houseplants such as rubber plants, palms, Norfolk Island pines, dragon trees or screw-pines. Small-leaved plants like indoor vines or weeping figs look good in a more modern room.

The most recent architecture, too, has its own requirements. The bold lines of the latest interiors create the ideal setting for the well-defined shapes of plants with dramatic foliage such as palms, crotons, *Dieffenbachia* or the Swiss cheese plant. Most of these look best against a plain, lightly coloured background. Large leaves can also compete with patterned wallpaper, provided they are big enough to contrast with the design. A plant that has many colours or a strong leaf structure

4

can create a sense of confusion if it is set against a bold, colourful design.

You needn't spend all your time extending and refining the choice of plants in your home.

It is far more important to create a well-balanced setting. Try to be influenced less by fashion and more by the need to incorporate your plants into a living environment. Living with plants is the object of the exercise.

Plants are essentially a part of nature. Like people, they depend on the processes that enable natural growth and development. In the wild, plants are directly affected by the rhythms of nature — the alternating patterns of day and night, warmth and cold, dryness and humidity, storm and calm, and the presence or absence of nutrients. Even inside the home plants remain sensitive to these rhythms. They are reflected in every stage of development: growth, flowering, fruiting, the sprouting of young shoots and the fall of older foliage. Real success with houseplants depends on understanding one simple rule. Your home must suit your choice of plants as much as the plants themselves suit your home.

Every home is different, and each home clearly reflects its owner's attitude to plants.

Light

If plants are to flourish, light is particularly important. Without light they can never survive in the long term. The green parts of the plant need light as an energy source to build up their organic tissue.

Depending on their country of origin, houseplants need very different amounts of light. Some like a great deal of sunlight, and will only thrive in a very sunny spot on a patio or in a sunlit room. These include nearly all the succulents and many plants with brightly coloured leaves. Other plants (e.g. flamingo flowers, ivies, indoor ferns and aspidistras) are only happy in partial or even total shade.

The unit of measurement for light falling on a surface is the lux, and it is based on the sensitivity of the human eye. If plants are to develop a little in winter as well as in summer they will need between 500 and 1,500 lux, depending on the species.

It is worth noting that a plant just 3 feet (1 m) away from a window receives only half the light it would receive on the window sill. The light conditions in a room can also vary enormously depending on the number of windows, their size and their positioning, not to mention curtains and other drapery. The direction a window faces can also be decisive.

In rooms with little or no natural light, some artificial lighting is essential. As a general guide, you will need a lamp producing about 250 W/m^2 and positioned about 5 ft (1.5 m) above the plant. A strategically placed halogen lamp should suit the purpose.

To sum up: don't just position your houseplants according to the architectural demands of the room; always make sure the light conditions are right for the plant.

Plants that need a lot of light: cacti, palm lilies (*Yucca*), screw-pines, cyclamens, *Aralia elegantissima*, gardenias, *Brunfelsia*, euphorbias, *Cordyline*, winter-flowering begonias, artillery plant, flowering maples, Norfolk Island pine, cycads, papyrus and silk oak (*Grevillia robusta*).

Plants that also flourish in the shade: rubber plant, Swiss cheese plant, *Epipremnum*, *Philodendron*, ivy, Chinese evergreen (*Aglaonema*), spider plant, indoor vine, indoor fern, aspidistra, *Aucuba*, aralia, parlour palm, kentia palm and some bromeliads.

Plants that are particularly sensitive to light (cuttings, for example) should be covered with tissue paper around midday. If the sun becomes too hot, you can move plants from the window sill into the middle of the room.

*Both these plants need plenty of light. On the left is the ponytail plant (*Beaucarnea recurvata*), and on the right the indoor azalea Rhododendron simsii.*

Temperature

Most houseplants are raised in greenhouses and come from areas with a variety of different climates — hence the variation in their temperature requirements. Before choosing a particular plant, find out what temperature it prefers. Plants that like a cool environment will not do well in an overheated room, whereas many tropical plants will become stunted in a cool environment.

The effects of light and temperature are interrelated. The warmer a room is, the more light you will need. Houseplants should never be kept in temperatures above 75°F (24°C), or they will need more light than a room can provide. Unless your home is connected

to a local or a district heating system, you will also need to prevent the temperature from falling too low, for instance when you are out at work. In general plants should never be kept at temperatures below 59°F (15°C), unless they actually prefer a cool environment. The cyclamen, for example, does well in a cool, airy northerly situation without too much direct sunlight.

It is also vital to avoid any large or sudden changes of temperature. All plants should be protected from cold draughts, especially in winter.

Plants in the middle of a room should always be shade-loving varieties such as the spider plant (Chlorophytum) and the flamingo flower (Anthurium–Scherzerianum hybrids). You can always use a lamp to provide some additional light.

Remember that most houseplants can die from the cold even at temperatures above freezing point.

7

Water

For houseplants, too much water is often more of a problem than too little. It is true that they cannot survive without water, but most plant lovers tend to drown their plants. This dilutes the essential nutrients, and prevents the roots from breathing.

There are times of the year when plants want more water and times when they want less. A plant needs water most when it is growing or in bloom. It needs less water in winter, when growth is much reduced, and immediately after pruning: because its leaves now have a smaller surface area, less moisture is lost through evaporation. If you continue to give it the same amount of water, the roots consequently will start to rot.

The roots will also rot if excess water cannot drain away. Putting a few pebbles or pot fragments at the bottom of the pot will prevent soil from blocking the drainage hole. If plants are placed directly into a decorative outer pot, they will effectively become water plants: excess water has no chance to drain away unless you put in some pebbles first.

Giving plants the right amount of water is largely a matter of fine judgement. Don't water them too often; in fact you can even allow the soil to dry out between waterings. On the other hand, never wait until the leaves start to droop. When watering your plants, make sure that the soil is thoroughly wetted. It isn't enough just to wet the surface. Some plants (such as cyclamens, gloxinias and African violets) should be watered from below.

Plants with thick, fleshy leaves generally need less water than those with soft shoots. The latter cannot store much water, and lose more through evaporation.

Bromeliads benefit from regular spraying rather than watering, because most of their moisture is absorbed from the centre of the leaf rosettes.

Humidity

Dry air is a problem for most indoor plants, and you should always bear this in mind when making your choice. We are often told that air in the average home is much drier than it used to be. The main reason for this is probably the disappearance of coal fires and stoves, although better night-time heating and draughtproof windows may also have played their part.

However, it is not difficult to improve the humidity of the air around your plants. One solution is to put the plants in a tub containing tree-bark, clay granules or a similar potting mixture. If you have central heating, hang humidifiers on all your radiators, and spray your plants from time to time. Wash dust off the leaves regularly (unless it's a plant with hairy leaves, such as saintpaulia). This allows the plants to absorb more moisture, and it will also boost the humidity of the surrounding air. You can even create a humid microclimate around your plants by placing the pots on trays full of damp gravel. Another way of doing this is to place each pot in a dish of water, using an upturned saucer to raise the pot clear of the water surface.

Most houseplants benefit from daily spraying with lukewarm water. As well as promoting growth this will stop the leaf tips turning brown.

The right nutrients

Air, water and light are all essential for plants to grow, but they are not enough on their own. Plants also need certain chemical elements — the so-called plant nutrients. The most important of these are nitrogen, phosphorus and potassium. Nitrogen is vital to leaf formation. Phosphorus helps root formation, and the development of flowers, fruits and seeds. Potassium is equally responsible for flower and fruit formation, but also improves the plant's resistance to disease. All these elements are part of a complex chain of biochemical reactions that enables a plant to flourish.

Most of these nutrients occur naturally in the soil, but with houseplants there can be problems. The small amount of material in the pot will only be able to provide nutrients for a few months. Of course, you can always feed them with a balanced houseplant fertiliser, but I prefer to repot the plants as soon as their roots are properly established, using fresh, nutritious, prefertilised soil.

Not all plants can stand this treatment. Palms, for example, never enjoy continual repotting. By contrast, I've had great success with scented geraniums, papyrus, *Datura* and many other tub plants, as long as they don't become too large and difficult to handle. I have noticed that thin-leaved plants that sprout quickly react much better to repotting than thick-leaved plants, such as the rubber plant (*Ficus elastica*) or *Schefflera* species.

The right time to feed your plants will depend on the season, the weather conditions and the plant's stage of development. Apply most of your fertiliser during the main growth period, which starts in the early spring and lasts well into August. The more luxuriant

*This grape ivy (*Rhoicissus rhomboidea*) has clearly been starved of nutrients, especially nitrogen. If the plant had been properly fed, it would have glossy, dark-green leaves.*

the plant growth, the more nutrients it will need, and the more fertiliser you can apply. However, too much feeding can be as bad as too little. The plants may become vulnerable to disease, and they can look as unsightly as if they had been starved of nutrients. The rule, once again, is 'little and often'.

If possible, fertilisers should be applied in liquid form. Plants that have just been repotted shouldn't need any feeding: the new soil should provide enough nutrients for the first month or so. Wait until the roots are fully established, and then start fertilising at fortnightly intervals.

When flowering plants are in bloom, use a high-potash feed such as tomato fertiliser.

11

Soil

Good soil provides four important things that any plant will need: adequate supplies of **air**, **water** and **nutrients**, and of course **stability**. These requirements are met by most of the potting composts sold today, including the various specialised forms. Potting soils for palms and cacti contain more sand and less humus than the others. There are also a number of highly acidic peat mixtures designed specially for azaleas and other ericaceous plants that don't like lime in the soil.

If you have your own garden, you can make up your own potting mixtures. A good homegrown compost is not easy to produce, but it can compete with any expensive mixture available over the counter. The best starting point is a good compost heap in which all the organic garden and kitchen waste has been well rotted down. A shredder can be used to reduce anything too large to decompose easily.

Animal manure, whether from cattle or from smaller animals, makes a good fertiliser, but don't put it straight into your potting compost. Mix it with your garden compost and leave it for at least a year.

Leaf compost, which is rich in humus, consists for the most part of decomposed beech leaves, mixed with those of other trees. It is well suited to most houseplants.

Lawn compost can be made using the grass mowings from lawns. It should ideally be mixed with animal manure and then left a long time so it can decompose properly. It can then be used for plants that require feeding with a lot of nutrients. Lawn compost is particularly good for plants such as oleanders, rubber plants, *Datura* and *Dieffenbachia* species.

Needle compost is obtained from the surface soils of coniferous forests, which are largely made up of decomposed material. This substrate is highly acidic, but contains few nutrients. It is good for azalias, African violets, camellias etc.

Tree-bark compost is yet another woodland product. It is made from shredded bark, usually taken from pine trees. This loose compost reduces decomposition and contains a lot of air. Because it does not retain water very well, it should only be used in combination with other potting composts and must be properly prepared first.

You can produce different kinds of potting compost by mixing ordinary garden soil with carefully measured quantities of sand, polystyrene chips and/or decomposed waste according to requirements.

You should only add small amounts of **loam** to your potting mixture. It tends to prevent air from getting to the roots, though it does contain large amounts of water and nutrients. Bonsai plants in particular will benefit from larger amounts of loam.

Peat, as ever, remains the most valuable potting material for house plants, especially in the earlier stages of growth. However, there are sound ecological reasons for limiting its use. Peat is a natural resource that is rapidly becoming depleted. Gardening suppliers, too, have responded to this problem by providing a choice of environmentally friendly alternatives. Like needle compost, peat contains few plant nutrients. Its main purpose is to increase the acidity of the soil.

Sand is yet another vital element of many potting composts. Cacti and other succulent plants need a large amount of sand, for example. Potting composts for palms also contain a little sand. Sand improves air circulation and water drainage, but it is extremely poor in nutrients.

Charcoal should also be mentioned here. Its antibacterial properties make it good for healing wounds when propagating plants. It is also used for the bottom layer in a bottle garden.

Finally, **molehills** can be a good source of fine-grained soil for use in sowing. Despite appearances, though, such soil is very poor in nutrients.

I use polystyrene chips when potting plants that prefer a light, well-drained soil. Just crumble up a little of this packing material and mix it into the compost. I use one handful for every 9 pt (5 l) of soil.

The right pot

Despite the many other pot materials available these days, earthenware pots seem to be making a come-back. They are heavy and they are liable to break, but they do have many advantages that are now being appreciated. Earthenware allows more moisture to evaporate, so you will need to water your plants more often. On the other hand, you can water them at longer intervals than plants in plastic pots, where overwatering can unfortunately have serious consequences.

The warm brown tints of these outer pots, made of stoneware, glazed earthenware or china, look attractive in themselves and are kind to the plants.

I think the final choice is a purely personal matter. Earthenware plant pots are attractive items even on their own. Plastic pots, unless they already have a decorative design, seem to cry out for some kind of outer pot (usually porcelain).

Whatever pot you choose, it should fulfil a few basic requirements. It must be stable, it must be large enough for the plant to root properly, and it must have at least one opening that allows water to escape. Plastic pots come with several different designs at the base, so check them carefully if you intend to put them in an outer pot or a saucer of water.

Sometimes there is a protruding rim that stops the water being absorbed. An indoor tree is invariably more stable in an earthenware pot than in a plastic one.

The outer pot is visually important: the right choice can provide the perfect foil for the plant it contains. Personally I like white porcelain: I think it can enhance the beauty of any plant. A simple, unadorned pot lets the plant speak for itself. However, there are other ways to make the colour of your pot work for the plant. You could, for example, choose a colour that matches part of the plant — the flowers or even (e.g. with the flame nettle) the leaves.

Tub plants such as citrus or oleander bushes look good in a simple earthenware or

terracotta pot. There is nothing to beat a large display of marguerites in a terracotta tub. Porcelain is more suited to the gentle grace of the smaller flowering plants such as cyclamens, primulas, wax plants and the like. Palms look good in pots of any material.

When buying an outer pot, try to keep it in style with the rest of the room. It should be large enough to let you slide your thumb between the inner and outer pots; this allows a little air to circulate. The edge of the inner pot should be just hidden by the outer pot. If the outer pot is of the right width but a little too tall, you can raise it a little by putting an upturned saucer or jam-jar lid underneath it.

Baskets or wooden tubs can also be used to great effect, but

Outer pots made of white porcelain have been popular for years because they enhance the beauty of the plants they contain.

remember that they are likely to get damp. It's advisable to line this kind of container with waterproof plastic or waxed cloth, and to take your lining about a third of the way up the side.

15

This plant is potbound and needs to be repotted as soon as possible.

Add a proper drainage layer to the bottom of the new pot, using pebbles and gravel.

Repotting

Plants generally grow so fast that their roots soon fill the pot. You should therefore pot on all your houseplants they have become established in their pots, preferably in the spring. Use a pot about 1 inch (2–3 cm) larger than the previous one. Palms are a notable exception: they like to grow 'right out of the pot', and only need repotting at 3–4 year intervals. Elderly rubber trees are a similar case: keep them in their pots, simply loosen the upper soil layers and replace them with fresh soil.

Repotting itself will inevitably affect the growth of the plant, but if you work carefully your plant will soon recover.

I have found this to be the best way of working:

■ Before repotting, put the plant in a bowl filled to the brim with water. Leave it for a few hours so the root ball is completely saturated.

■ Make sure the new pot has a proper drainage hole, and put a few pebbles or potsherds in the bottom. Spread enough soil in the bottom to cover the base.

■ Support the plant with your hand around the base of the stem, and gently ease it out of the old pot. Strip the root ball of any old, rotten roots; these are normally dark brown and unpleasant-smelling.

■ Place the root ball in the middle of the new pot, first adding a little extra soil to the base of the pot if necessary. Fill the pot with the new soil using your free hand, pressing it down

st cover the base with a little soil — use just enough to e the root ball sufficient room.

Place the plant in the middle of the new pot, and fill up with soil.

firmly. Water the plant carefully with just a little water.

■ Place the newly repotted plant in a warm, sheltered position. This will help it to overcome the shock more quickly. The growth of new shoots will indicate that it is comfortable in its new environment.

When you have finished, water the plant very carefully.

Tools and other basic necessities

If you are really serious about houseplants you will need some tools and a few basic necessities — and you should begin with a good book about houseplants! The photographs will help you to identify any new plants that you buy, and the text will give you useful tips on looking after them.

You will often find basic information about the plant on a plastic tag stuck in the soil around it. However, this is frequently very superficial and may even contain errors of fact.

Always buy your plants from a specialist gardening shop or gardening centre, and ask for the appropriate advice at the same time. This is the only way to be reasonably certain that the new plant will thrive in your home.

Once you are fully informed about the plant, and know something about its habits and its needs, there are a number of tools and other basic necessities that you are likely to need:

- soil (potting compost) for repotting plants
- a watering can with a long spout so that you can get at the plants properly
- a plant sprayer for sprinkling plants with lukewarm water (most plants will benefit from this)
- an indoor thermometer
- a pair of pruning shears
- a selection of plant pots

- wire and string to tie up your plants
- bamboo canes and loop wire for helping to shape plants
- a good liquid fertiliser, ideally containing guano (phosphate) and plenty of organic ingredients (don't go for the cheapest — quality is important)
- some large glass tumblers or plastic bags to create a humid microclimate for young plants
- ground charcoal to rub into wounds; this will stop decay when you are taking cuttings
- a universal pest repellent, ideally one that is environmentally friendly.

From experience you will gradually learn which of these items you need and which you can manage without. Only the absolute essentials are listed here. You could, for example, collect rubber rings and plastic food containers, which you could then recycle for sowing seedlings. A sieve is a basic essential for growing from seed, when fine sieving is required.

As far as the tools are concerned, it doesn't really matter whether they are old-fashioned or up-to-date. The important thing is that they work properly. A knife has to be sharp, and shears must be capable of shearing. A watering

can needs a spout that is long enough to reach the centre of any plant, and a rod must be strong enough not to bend.

Tools should be kept scrupulously clean at all times. This prevents diseases from being carried from one plant to another. It also avoids the risk that plants such as oleanders and *Dieffenbachia* may leave poisonous substances on your tools. If a tool isn't thoroughly cleaned after every job, it is so easy to cause inflammations by inadvertently rubbing your eyes or mouth; your hands are vulnerable, too.

Make sure your watering can is big enough, so you aren't for ever running to the tap. You should always let the water stand for a while before using it.

Houseplants are easy to care for with the right tools and a few basic necessities.

Plants without soil

It's actually possible to grow plants without soil, using a method known as *hydroponics*. Hydroponics replaces the nutrient-rich, water-bearing soil with a nutritious watery solution.

The technique has a number of advantages. You don't need to water the plants every day, and you don't have to apply fertiliser at weekly intervals during the main growth period. This makes holiday plant care a great deal easier, but there are other advantages. Houseplants raised hydroponically tend to grow more luxuriant, and are generally healthier and more resistant to disease.

The first thing is to create a substrate for the plants to root in. The usual materials for this are gravel, stone chippings, or granules of porous clay. You can even buy plastic materials that are suitable. Gravel gives the roots something solid to get hold of, while the more porous substrates allow better ventilation around the roots.

Essentially you need two pots to grow a plant hydroponically. The inner pot contains the substrate with the plant and its root system, and has holes in its base so the nutrient solution can be absorbed. The outer container can be decorative as well as functional — and if you

want to grow a whole collection of plants, you can use a hydroponic trough or tank as an outer container.

The nutrient solution is made up of water mixed with the appropriate quantity of the hydroponic solution. If your tap water is very hard or chalky, it's better to use rain water. You should replace the nutrient solution completely every eight weeks or so, and remove any salts that have leached out onto the roots and substrates by watering for half an hour. You can top up with pure water at other times, but don't add any

Expanded clay granules provide an excellent planting medium for growing plants hydroponically.

Think carefully before topping up with water or nutrient solution — too much of a good thing and the plants will suffer. The best advice is to keep to a strict routine.

more nutrient salts or the solution may become too concentrated. Between each watering the container should be allowed to dry out completely. It should be left dry for at least one week before replenishing.

If you want to transfer plants grown by conventional means into a hydroponic medium, do it in spring or summer. Take the plant carefully out of its pot, and tap it gently to remove the soil. Rinse the roots thoroughly in a large bowl of water (or under the tap), taking care not to damage them. Finally put the plant in the substrate.

In principle, hydroponics can work well for any plant, but some will manage better than others. The important thing is to keep the plants moist, with plenty of warmth from below. An ideal spot that should give marvellous results is on a window sill above a radiator. If your plants are kept too cool, the roots will tend to rot. Foliage plants are particularly suitable, notably the Swiss cheese plant, *Epipremnum*, philodendron, indoor vine, *Dieffenbachia*, screw-pine, dragon tree, rubber plant and some palm species.

If your plants are going through a dormant winter phase, keep the water level very low. With cacti, for example, you should only water the substrate once a fortnight during the period of lower temperatures. If the pot smells unpleasant the plant has probably been starved of oxygen. It may be that the nutrient solution should have been changed more often, or that the water level has been too high over a long period. The only treatment is to give the roots and substrate a thorough rinse, and then replace the nutrient medium.

The wrong treatment

Far left *Someone has simply forgotten to water this azalea (Rhododendron simsii).*
Above *Too much sunlight on this shade-loving parlour palm (Chamaedorea elegans) has caused leaf burns, which can quickly lead to fungal diseases such as rust mould.*

Pests and diseases usually appear when the growth of a plant has been disturbed in some way. A plant that is not given enough food and water, or receives too little light and heat, will become weak, and vulnerable to any pest it happens to encounter. But too *much* of anything — warmth, cold, fertiliser, sunlight, moisture or shade — can produce exactly the same result.

If you want to keep a plant healthy, you should keep all these factors in a careful balance according to the season and the species of plant. Success depends on knowing what each individual plant needs from its surroundings. Take just one example from my own garden. Rhododendrons usually prefer a half-shaded location, yet I have one plant that can stand in the sun all day long and will still grow and flower with the best

of them. Never think of any gardening rule as being written on tablets of stone. Plants are sensitive living things, and each of them reacts individually.

If the leaves of a plant drop off, or become yellowish at the tips, disease or infestation may not always be the problem. In azaleas, for example, these symptoms are often the result of **water deficiency**. Lack of water in budding cyclamens may cause the flowers to grow out of sight, under the leaves. Irregular watering of pelargoniums can cause the stems to break. Camellias will tend to lose their flower buds, while gloxinia leaves begin to curl. Papyrus quickly develops brown leaf spots if it doesn't get enough water.

Another closely related problem is **lack of humidity**; there are very few plants that like the dry air of centrally heated rooms.

Overwatering, however, is equally dangerous: the leaves go yellow, the roots begin to rot, and the plant gradually dies. Pot plants simply waste away.

Lack of warmth, especially over a long period, slows down plant growth and creates a breeding ground for fungal diseases. Flowers begin to drop off. If a mother-in-law's tongue (*Sansevieria*) is kept in damp soil at temperatures below 50°F (10°C), the leaves become soft and transparent and start to fall over. Gloxinias stop growing when the temperature drops below 59°C (15°C), while bud formation in azaleas is affected below 36°F (2°C). **Too much warmth** can be just as damaging.

If there is **too much light** the leaves become spotted with burns, and have to be removed. Overexposure to intense sunlight produces red-brown discoloration on cacti, *Kalanchoe* and Lorraine begonias. You can reduce the damaging effects of the midday sun by covering plants on a window sill with tissue paper, or a similar translucent material.

If there is **too little light** even the stockiest plant will become tall and thin, and its leaves will turn a light green. This 'lean and hungry' look is particularly common in winter, and excessive warmth can make it even more pronounced.

*This piggyback plant (*Tolmiea menziesii*) has clearly been starved of nutrients and exposed to extreme changes of temperature.*

Fungal diseases

Houseplants are very frequently attacked by fungal diseases. **Grey mould**, which is often seen on strawberry plants in wet weather, is encouraged by damp, stagnant air. The fungus forms a furry grey-brown mould on the leaves, buds and shoots, and basically causes the plant to rot.

As an initial remedy, improve the ventilation around the plant. Move it well away from its neighbours and cut out the diseased parts. Take great care to prevent the spores from spreading to other, healthy parts of the plant. Before putting it back on a window sill, give both the window and the window sill a thorough wipe to remove any remaining spores. Finally, make sure that it isn't standing too close to other plants.

Fungal infections seem to have a particular liking for soft-leaved plants such as members of the Gesneriaceae family: gloxinias, African violets, hot water plants and Cape primroses. Other similarly vulnerable plants include fuchsias, azaleas and primulas.

Rust mould creates circular reddish-brown spots on the leaves. It is common on palms, where it eventually causes the leaves to drop off and the leaf shoots to become deformed. Pelargonias, cinerarias, heaths and fuchsias are similarly liable to rust mould. The best remedy is to cut out the affected leaves.

Houseplants can suffer from a whole series of so-called **blackleg diseases**. The offending fungi live in the soil, feeding on rotting vegetable matter, and they thrive in stagnant wet conditions. They attack the roots and the base of the stem, causing the whole plant to turn yellow and wilt. The stem eventually rots right through. Begonias, cinerarias, African violets and *Kalanchoe*

Fungal diseases can also make the leaves curl up, as on this flowering maple (Abutilon hybrid).

are particularly vulnerable. The best way to prevent blackleg disease is to avoid the conditions that cause it. When you're repotting a plant, don't forget to line the base of the pot with a drainage layer made up of pebbles or pot fragments. This ensures that your plant will always be properly drained. And do make sure that the plant is not too low in the soil.

A regular dose of fertiliser can also help prevent fungal infesta-tion — and provided you don't let the temperature fall too low, your plants should remain healthy, strong and resistant to all these diseases.

All fungal infections can be treated chemically, using a range of fungicides. But it's much better to improve the conditions in the first place. Chemical treatments are difficult to apply in the home, and should only be thought of as a last resort.

The rust spots on this Swiss cheese plant (Monstera deliciosa) look like burns, but they are mainly caused by inappropriate treatment.

One way to avoid blackleg disease is to ensure sure that when you repot a plant it is always in the same position relative to the soil as it was in the old pot.

Pests

Plants can become a home for a variety of insect pests. **Aphids**, for example, are small and soft-skinned; some have wings and some do not, depending on the species. The species name often reflects the colour (e.g. greenfly and blackfly). In extreme cases the leaves will curl up and the

---

There are several recipes for making liquid manure from stinging nettles. My own involves harvesting about 2 lb (1 kg) of stinging nettles, complete with stems and leaves, just before they flower. I chop them roughly with a knife and add about 18 pt (10 l) of water. (Don't use a metal container, as it will be attacked by the liquid.) After about 12–24 hours the manure should be strong enough to spray over the affected plants.

---

leaf shoots will become deformed.

Repeated spraying with water can do a lot to remove aphids. A soap solution can also be very effective. A good long-term treatment is a liquid manure made from stinging nettles; this can actually protect the plants against infestation. Frequent doses will make the plant so strong that the aphids have little chance of attacking it.

Scale insects form small, shield-like growths on a plant. They are soft and light-coloured at first, but gradually become brown and hard. If the infesta-tion, is serious the leaves will discolour and eventually fall off.

The usual treatment for scale is simply to scrape it off. Before you start, however, place a piece of paper or foil over the soil and close around the stem of the plant. This is to catch the actual insects that lurk under-neath the scale: if these fall onto the soil they will simply re-colonise the plant. Washing the plant with a weak soap solution can also help.

Unlike aphids, scale insects are not confined to soft-leaved plants. On the contrary, they are particularly fond of the more hard-leaved species such as palms, camellias, agaves, oleanders and flamingo flowers.

Mealy bugs secrete a waxy whitish or grey-coloured substance that looks like cotton wool. They like to settle at the bases of leaves, and multiply very quickly. Like scale they cause leaf discoloration; later growth is stunted, and the leaves will eventually fall. Mealy bugs have a special affinity for cacti, palms and ferns.

As soon as you discover mealy bugs, you should remove them and pluck off the woolly secretions with a paintbrush soaked in edible oil. This effectively suffocates the bugs.

Thrips are tiny black-winged insects. Their young larvae can be found on the underside of leaves. The fully grown larvae will infest the whole plant, causing whitish spots (especially in a warm, dry room). Later on, the leaves will turn yellow.

This pest can be removed by shaking the plant over a piece of paper so that the insects fall

A home-made liquid fertiliser produced from stinging nettles can be used for as long as you like, although it loses its effectiveness as an aphid repellent within two days of its manufacture.

Aphids

A whitefly infestation

Scale insects are hidden under shield-like scales. Take great care when removing these pests.

Mealy bugs can be 'suffocated' using a paintbrush soaked in edible oil.

A parlour palm infested with red spider mites.

off. Thrips are common on cyclamens, flamingo flowers, pelargoniums, ornamental asparagus and begonias. Badly affected plants should be destroyed.

Red spider mites are related to spiders rather than insects. These tiny creatures feed on the sap of a variety of plants. Because they reproduce very quickly, spider mites are the commonest and most widespread of all houseplant pests anywhere in the world.

At first, infested leaves will develop yellowish-white speckles on their upper surfaces. Later they will turn yellow and fall off. Some plants turn brown, while some leaves take on a silvery-grey sheen caused by air getting into the exhausted plant cells.

Spider mites multiply by laying eggs: these can be seen as tiny whitish-yellow balls at the bases of the leaves. They like a warm, dry environment, so infested plants should be washed with soap solution, sprayed regularly, and kept in a slightly cooler, damper location.

Growing plants from seed

Many pot plants are easy to propagate from seed, among them cyclamens, primulas, ornamental *Capsicum* peppers, slipper flowers, begonias and cacti. The potting mixture should be a very light, sandy soil; ideally it should be sterilised before you start. One way of doing this is to bake the soil in a preserving jar. Leave the uncovered jar in an oven preheated to more than 212°F (100°C) and it will be sterilised in about half an hour. Once the soil has cooled down you can put it out in your seed trays, and you're ready to begin sowing.

The seeds should normally be covered with a layer of fine, sandy soil. As a rule of thumb, this layer should usually be about as deep as the size of the seed. However, small seeds (like those of primulas and slipper

flowers) should not be covered, but simply pressed into the soil.

Hard seeds (e.g. palms) should be soaked for 24 hours in warm water before sowing. A quicker alternative is to scratch them carefully with a nail file. Large seeds (e.g. avocado plants) should be one-third submerged in a container of water.

After sowing, cover the seed trays with a sheet of glass or transparent plastic and leave them in a warm place. Take off the cover when the first leaves appear. As soon as the second set of leaves has sprouted the plants are ready to be pricked out, or planted separately. At this stage you can, if you wish, plant them in a large bowl, or in the flower pot you have selected for them. Don't, however, use sandy soil — it needs to be full of nutrients. Be extremely careful when removing the young seedlings: loosen the roots with a wooden dibber before taking each plant out of the soil and lift by the leaves, not by the stem.

Before you replant the seedling, smooth off the soil in the

new pot and make a small hole with your finger or with the dibber. It should be just deep enough to cover the roots. After planting, gently press the soil down around the seedling with two fingers. Give the plant a final watering; it usually perks up within a day, especially if you put a piece of glass over the pot.

> Let the seedling dry out for a day or two before pricking it out. This will ensure that the soil crumbles easily and the root comes out in one piece. However, do give the plant a good watering as soon as you've finished pricking out.

Care is the watchword when pricking out or separating seedlings. The tiny, delicate roots must not be damaged!

Vegetative propagation

Many houseplants are difficult to grow from seed, unless you're prepared to give them a lot of care and effort. In such cases the best solution is vegetative propagation in the spring or summer. Various parts of the plant can be used, including sections of the trunk or stem, the roots, single leaves or even pieces of leaf.

Many plants throw out shoots and form new plantlets at the end of them. The spider plant, the mother of thousands and the piggyback plant all propagate themselves in this way. Other genera and species have tubers that can be divided, or bulbs that produce **offsets** (small replicas of themselves). Examples include rosary vines, hot water plants, begonias, hyacinths and amaryllis (*Hippeastrum* hybrids).

Very often plants can be propagated from a **stem cutting**. This consists of the end of a shoot together with two or three full-grown leaves or leaf pairs. Do ensure there are no flower buds on the cutting, or it won't take root. You should also limit the amount of moisture lost through the leaves, which is why two leaf pairs should be enough for rooting. Thick, fleshy stems should be dusted with charcoal powder.

Some plants will even root if you put a cutting in a glass of water — among them oleanders, spider plants, lemon geraniums, passion flowers and indoor vines. Otherwise the cuttings should always be planted in a moist potting mixture with very few nutrients, and placed in a warm, sheltered location. As with sowing, it's a

Remove a stem cutting from the parent plant using a clean knife. Make sure the cutting includes at least one pair of leaves. Cuttings from most houseplants will form roots if they are left in a glass of water.

good idea to cover the plant with a clear plastic bag or a glass tumbler.

The simplest method of propagation is to use **leaf cuttings**. Some plants can even develop new plantlets from a tiny piece of leaf — a process that is familiar in the chandelier plant (*Bryophyllum tubiflorum*). With the African violet and Cape primrose you can simply

Just push a few African violet leaves (Saintpaulia ionantha) into the soil, and the new plantlets will soon emerge.

The Lorraine begonia will grow from small leaves, each with a section of stem, planted flat and fairly close together in an earthenware bowl filled with sand. Leaf propagation of the fan begonia (*Begonia rex*) is particularly interesting. Choose a leaf that is not too old from the parent plant and make a few slits through the leaf ribs, at an angle to the main veins. Three-quarters fill a bowl with loose, damp soil. Lay the leaf underside-down on the soil, putting tiny stones over the slits so their edges touch the damp

take a leaf and push its stem into warm soil. You will soon see a new plantlet growing where the stem has been buried.

Peperomia can be propagated from individual leaf cuttings in much the same way. In this case, however, you should keep the whole leaf stem and plant it upright in a pot with other cuttings of the same plant. In warm, moist conditions the leaf cuttings will take root.

A controlled microclimate is always good for young plants. This simple propagator box provides the ideal conditions and plenty of humidity for the young seedlings and plantlets.

soil. Finally, lay a sheet of glass over the bowl, and put it in a very warm but fairly shady place. Water the plants only from below, or they will rot. Once they are sufficiently well rooted, and the plantlets are strong enough, you can divide them and prick out each plantlet in a separate pot together with the piece of leaf from which it grew.

The mother-in-law's tongue (*Sansevieria*) can also be propagated using leaf sections — simply take a well-developed leaf and chop it into 2-inch (5-cm) pieces. The yellow-margined 'Laurentii' form will, however, lose its yellow colouration and revert to the original green.

Cuttings from plants with very fleshy leaves — for example, cacti and other succulents, or the leaf rosettes of pineapples — should first be dried off in a shady place to prevent them from rotting. The cutting can be planted after a couple of days provided the cut edge or break point is fully dried out. Because such cuttings have leaves but no roots, it is vital to minimise water loss through evaporation until the cutting has dried out. A leaf cutting from a rubber plant, for example, should be rolled up and secured with a rubber band.

Newly propagated plantlets are invariably more sensitive than their properly rooted parent plants. That's why I always put them in a warm, sheltered place and keep them moist all the time. It's usually a good idea to put a plastic bag or a piece of glass over the young plant.

Some plants, including papyrus and ferns, can be propagated by **division** when you are repotting them. Again, extreme care is vital, and you will sometimes need a sharp knife.

Plants like the mother of thousands and the spider plant propagate themselves naturally by means of **shoots and plantlets**. The 'baby' plants can be left to root in a glass of water, or you can plant them in damp soil straight away.

Tubers such as those of tuberous begonias should be cut into pieces. Make sure each piece includes at least one eye, and then plant them in separate pots to produce new plants.

When you're taking leaf cuttings from large-leaved plants such as the rubber plant (Ficus elastica), roll the leaf up gently. This is a great help in persuading the plant to root.

If a rubber plant grows up to the ceiling you can cut off the top in the summer and grow a new plant from the cutting. A large cutting like this is best propagated by a process known as **air layering**. If you want to try this, make sure your plant is growing strongly and has a large number of leaves.

Find the fourth leaf pair down from the top, and place a sharp knife just below the leaf node. Make a careful cut through the middle of the stem, starting horizontally and gradually turning the knife upwards. Use a wooden spill to hold the stem open where it has been cut. Now take a fistful of really wet moss, and wrap it closely around the wound and the leaf stem. Press the moss together and wrap it tightly in polythene to create a watertight parcel. Bind the package to the plant stem with raffia both above and below the cut, and keep it moist all the time. It's a good idea to tie the weakened stem to a stout cane to prevent it breaking.

After about six weeks the plant will develop roots at the point where it has been cut. The newly rooting top shoot can then be removed from its parent plant by cutting below the break point. Pot it straight away, making sure there is plenty of humus in the soil. If a new leaf shoot appears, the new plant is growing well.

Grafting is yet another method of propagation, and one that's especially useful for cacti. Some cacti root badly or grow

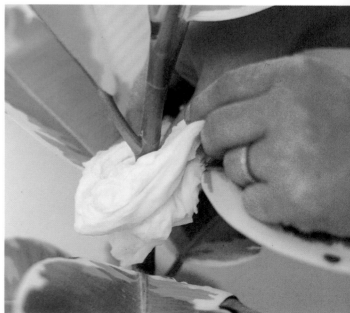

very slowly, and it may be hard to persuade them to flower. Grafting is a very effective way of speeding up their growth and making them flower sooner. The taller base can often enable the plant to grow at twice its normal speed — and grafting has saved many a cactus with a damaged or diseased base.

A good time for grafting is a period of warm, dry weather in summer. The best **grafting stock** (base plant) will come from one of the faster-growing cacti such as *Cereus* species, or from columnar cacti which don't produce many side

Air layering is a technique that demands the utmost cleanliness. The first roots form at the cutting point after about six weeks.

shoots. The only equipment you need is a thin, sharp knife, a pair of tweezers, some rubber bands and a cloth.

Cut the grafting stock at the point where the fresh, green shoot from the previous year began to grow. You should cut horizontally through the plant, working from the handle of the knife towards the blade; this cut should be within the top third of the plant, at a height of about 2 inches (5 cm). File off the areoles (the tiny shoots from which the spines grow) at the top of the base to prevent any side shoots from appearing at this point.

The **scion** — the plant you want to graft onto the base — should also be freshly cut. Place the cut end of the scion over

Rubber plants are the usual candidates for air layering, but parlour palms can also be propagated this way. Rubber plants produce a lot of sticky white sap, so always be sure to wash your hands thoroughly.

the wound on the grafting stock so that the two sections are in direct contact. A slight turn and a little gentle pressure will remove any remaining air bubbles between them.

The whole process must be carried out swiftly, and with scrupulous attention to cleanliness. You should clean and dry the knife after every cut, disinfecting it with an alcohol solution. Now secure the graft with the rubber bands. Draw the first band down under the bottom of the pot, stretch it up over the plant, and slide it carefully down over the top of the scion. Attach a second band in the same way, but at right angles to the first.

Keep your grafted cacti somewhere dry but not too sunny, at a temperature of about 75-85°F (25-30°C). Water them very carefully for the first two weeks: make sure the graft point never comes into contact with any water. Once the fortnight is up, you can take off the rubber bands.

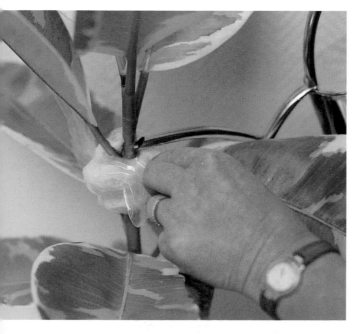

Homegrown tropical fruits

It's tempting to experiment with the stones or other parts of tropical fruits available in the shops. Even under normal room conditions this can produce some magnificent houseplants. Admittedly they demand a lot of patience at the sowing stage because they often take a long time to germinate. And don't count on a tasty fruit harvest; to achieve that you'll often need specially grafted specimens, as you do for many of our indigenous fruit trees. Besides, in a home environment these plants probably won't become mature enough to produce fruit. Even so, growing tropical fruits can give you a great deal of pleasure. You'll already be familiar with the seeds and the fruits, but the plant and its foliage are an exotic experience in themselves.

The **pineapple plant** (*Ananas comosus*) belongs to the bromeliad family. Its leaf rosettes make it very attractive, and it can easily be cultivated from part of the fruit. Cut off the top part of the pineapple together with about 1 inch (3 cm) of the flesh. Pare away the flesh as far as the hard, fibrous section in the middle. Leave this section exposed to the air for about three days: this allows it to dry out, and prevents it from rotting. Now remove the bottom leaves and plant the pineapple in a humous, sandy potting mixture. Keep the pot in a warm, well-lit place, but try to prevent the mixture from becoming too moist.

An **avocado bush** (*Persea americana*) can be grown very simply from a fruit stone. It's important to start by inserting four wooden toothpicks at equal intervals into the side of the stone. This will allow you to support the stone over a glass filled with water so that its lower portion is submerged. You'll find that the stone already has enough nutrients inside it to grow roots, shoots and leaves. As soon as there are enough roots, take out the matches and pot the stone in soil.

You can grow a highly decorative **coffee bush** (*Coffea arabica*) from a single unroasted coffee bean. If the bean is to germinate, it needs to be sown in a warm, moist potting mixture. Once the plant has developed, don't keep it too warm, and put it in a half-shaded location. The leaves are copper-coloured at first, but later they take on a dark-green sheen. Small, white, sweet-

This avocado plant can now be pruned. This will encourage it to form branches and to grow more strongly.

smelling flowers are followed by the red berries that contain the coffee beans. The bush should be pruned a little; this will encourage branches to form.

An attractive **ginger plant** (*Zingiber officinale*) can be grown from a simple ginger root. Start by putting the rhizome in water so it will form roots, and then pot it in good

Even a young pineapple plant (Ananas comosus) can easily be recognised from its fruit.

soil and put it in a warm, humid, well-lit position. I have also tried potting the rhizome directly into wet soil and covering it completely with a glass — this, too, has been very successful.

You can even grow a **date palm** (*Phoenix dactylifera*) from a stone taken out of a packet of preserved dates. First let the stone germinate in water that is kept permanently warm, and then plant it in wet soil. As soon as the seedlings have grown a couple of leaves, repot the plant and keep it warm, moist and well lit. The plant will appear to become dormant for a while, but don't worry — there's always a delay before it finally decides to put out leaves.

Tall or bushy?

The rose of China (Hibiscus rosa-sinensis) *will remain bushy if it is pruned frequently — but wait until it has flowered properly for the first time.*

The daily care of houseplants involves more than just checking that they have enough water. There are other things to be done if you want to improve the natural growth potential of your plants, and ensure that they thrive and flourish.

By **topping** a young plant — cutting off the upper shoots while they are still soft — you can persuade it to form extra branches. This may be desirable, for example, with hibiscus, some pelargonium species (e.g. *Pelargonium graveolens*),

indoor vines (*Cissus*), oleanders (*Nerium*), creeping fig (*Ficus pumila*) and ivies in general. If you want a plant such as a myrtle to develop a particularly bushy habit, top it several times. It will develop more shoots, and ultimately more flowers.

It's worth noting that oleanders won't bloom in the first year after topping, although the foliage will benefit by becoming denser. Plants such as fuchsias can be topped to delay flowering, or to lengthen the flowering period.

Don't imagine that topping will weaken the growth of a plant that is growing too strongly. On the contrary, most plants react to trimming of any sort with renewed growth — and if anything it will be stronger than it was before.

There are any number of reasons for **pruning** houseplants. They may have grown unsightly. The lower parts may have become bare. Some plants (rubber plants, for instance) may simply grow too big for the room they're in.

CULTIVATION AND PROPAGATION

During the winter months there's less light available indoors. As a result many plants will produce weak, etiolated growth that doesn't do much for their appearance. In early spring it's a good idea to prune away this growth, along with anything else that looks untidy or unattractive, so the plants get off to a good start for the new season. A sharp pruning knife or sharp pruning shears are essential.

The growth pattern of a plant can be radically affected by pruning. Uneven growth can be evened out, and plants that are growing weakly because they are too close together can be distanced from each other.

If climbers such as the wax plant, passion flower, *Dipladenia* or jasmine aren't grown in a hanging basket, they'll need a **support** of some kind — probably a climbing frame or a pole fixed into the pot.

Climbers that come from tropical rain forests (*Philodendron*, for instance), like nothing better than a **moss stick** to climb up. A moss stick covered in greenery doesn't just look attractive; it also provides a ready source of moisture. If you spray or water it from above, it stores the moisture and lets it evaporate slowly, ensuring a continuous supply to the plants it is supporting. This method is particularly suitable for plants that form aerial roots or (as in the case of ivy) clinging roots.

Even large hanging plants can be transferred to a moss stick, although they will take some time to get used to their new climbing environment. Take great care when installing the pole: make sure you have a large enough pot, and gently loosen the roots of the plant to accommodate the pole in the middle.

You can buy a moss stick at any gardening outlet. Make sure you use a pot that is large enough to accommodate the stick, and bed it down firmly in the soil. Plant the climber in the same pot, and secure it to the lower part of the pole with fishing wire or some similar material. Keep both the soil and the pole continuously moist. As the plant grows it will climb up the pole, attracted by the moist environment that it finds there.

Epipremnum aureum or devil's ivy is ideally suited to a moss stick. Each new shoot should be gently wrapped around the pole and secured with raffia.

Standards

These miniature trees are enjoying increasing popularity as houseplants. With a little care and patience you can grow them at home, though you'll have to wait about five years before the plant develops a proper crown.

Any woody ornamental plant is suitable for this treatment. Examples include hibiscus, gardenia, pelargonium, myrtle, chrysanthemum, fuchsia, azalia, oleander, heliotrope, climbing rose, rosemary, citrus, flowering maple, laurel, plumbago (leadwort), weeping fig, *Schefflera* and many garden shrubs.

At first you should only allow the main shoot to grow, until it reaches the height that you want. If any side shoots appear, remove them at once. You'll probably need to support the plant with a stick. Once it reaches the proper height, cut off the top of the main shoot and allow the side shoots at the top to grow instead; give them support if they need it. This will form a crown. Meanwhile, keep cutting back any side shoots that appear lower down. Don't prune the crown unless you want to create a particular shape.

Standards are most effective when they stand alone, and most of them make an attractive addition to a patio, balcony or winter garden. One good arrangement for a room could involve surrounding a standard with smaller, bushier versions of the same plant, or pairing it with a low-growing plant such as mind your own business.

You can speed up the development of standards by giving them plenty of food and water during the growth phase. They also need to be kept in a warm, well-lit situation, though they should never be placed in direct sunlight.

Left *This weeping fig* (Ficus benjamina) *looks magnificent with its spiral trunk.* **Right** *A common hydrangea* (Hydrangea macrophylla) *can be turned into a standard in the space of a few years.*

What to do when you go on holiday

Every year when the holiday season looms you are faced with the problem of what to do with the houseplants. The best solution is to recruit willing friends or neighbours to take care of the watering. If this isn't possible, you must find some other way to prevent your plants from dying of thirst.

The notable exceptions to this are most of the succulents, especially cacti and the indestructible mother-in-law's tongue. Provided these are moved from a sunny position into the shade, they can survive as long as ten days without any additional watering.

In the summer many house-plants can manage very well over the holiday period in a sheltered, well-shaded part of the garden. With palms, rubber plants, large ivies, ferns and most other foliage plants the pot should be sunk into the soil a little. Pot plants with very soft and/or hairy leaves can't cope with the fresh air, and will soon rot if they're exposed to heavy rain. You'll need to consider other possibilities — and of course the same applies if you don't have a garden.

If you're only away for a few days, just water your plants thoroughly before you leave. If you're taking a longer holiday there's always the temptation to stand the plant pot in a dish of water to stop the soil drying out. This may do more harm than good: many plants actually benefit from being allowed to dry out at the roots occasionally.

If you're only away for a short time, you can stand your plant pots in a larger container filled with moist peat or sand.

A simple arrangement like this one can provide a continuous source of fresh water, but you should always check how to see how it works before going on holiday.

A better idea is to stand your plants on a bed of wet sand. Capillary action will then draw water up into the soil. Larger plants (or a larger collection) can be left in the bath. First line the bath with a polythene sheet. Now lay down a few inches of sand, ensuring it's well wetted. Finally press the base of each pot firmly into the sand —

you'll need to put a cotton wool plug into the holes at the bottom of clay pots, as there's no way moisture can bridge the gap.

Yet another method, involving lengths of wool, would have been familiar to our grandparents. First group your plant pots closer together around a bowl of water. Next, take a few lengths of thick wool and saturate them with water. Bury one end of each piece between the potting mixture and the wall of each pot, and put the other into your bowl of water. The wool creates a water channel between the bowl and the pot. This method doesn't always work, so be sure to test

out your irrigation system before you leave!

Houseplants growing in a hydroponic medium are much less of a problem at holiday time. If necessary they can be left unattended for at least four weeks as long as temperatures are adequate and they're not in direct sunlight (which tends to dry them out more quickly). Normally it's not a good idea to top up these containers, but before you leave do check that the filler gauge is at maximum. This should ensure the plants get enough moisture even during a long absence.

Whatever you decide to do, give all your plants a thorough watering before you leave.

Flowers from spring to autumn

Flowers in pots, like bunches of flowers, bring a splash of colour to any room. As these colours are usually conspicuous, and often intense, you need to think carefully about where you want to put them. Even if they are only placed somewhere for a short time — as a nice table decoration, for example — they should always fit in with their surroundings.

Many of the flowering plants you buy will be 'throw-aways'. Once they've flowered, it's no use trying to grow or propagate them any further. Simply pick a place where they will look attractive, and leave them there till they don't look attractive any more. By contrast, plants that grow and flower for many years should obviously be placed where the temperature and light conditions are right for them. Only then will they flourish properly.

Short-lived beauties

Primulas (including primroses) are among the most attractive pot plants that bloom in the late winter. They're a sign of approaching spring, and their soft yet bright tints can bring a touch of freshness to any window-sill. If they are well cared for, they will flower for many weeks. They should not, however, be kept too warm, and there should always be plenty of moisture.

Hardy primulas — those neat little flowers that bloom in the early spring — can be planted in the garden as soon as they have stopped flowering. They will bloom again within the year, and almost certainly the following year as well.

The **cineraria** (*Senecio–Cruentus* hybrids) comes into flower at the end of winter. Don't subject it to dry air or too much warmth. Hoards of aphids are the usual consequence — so much so that the plant has even been dubbed 'aphid blossom'. But the flowers make a lovely display.

The year's first primroses (Primula vulgaris) are always beautiful. They can be planted out in the garden as soon as they've finished flowering.

Regrettably, this pretty cineraria (Senecio–Cruentus hybrids) is one of those plants that isn't worth keeping. It can easily fall prey to aphids.

The indestructible **busy lizzie** (*Impatiens* hybrids) is a typical summer flower. Some magnificent varieties have appeared in recent years, showing a glorious interplay of colour between the flowers and leaves — hence their ever-increasing popularity. The name reflects this plant's inexhaustible capacity to produce flowers — and, what's more, they are flowers that last. These flowers develop particularly well if you leave the pot in the open air.

Although the busy lizzie will grow for several years, the stem tends to become bare as it gets older, so it's a good idea to take cuttings in the summer and repot them as soon as they have rooted. *Impatiens* can even

Above *The busy lizzie (Impatiens New Guinea hybrids) comes in a wide range of varieties. It can effectively be 'rejuvenated' by propagation from cuttings.*

cope with full sunlight provided it has become acclimatised, but don't forget to feed and water it well.

The **slipper flower** (*Calceolaria* hybrids) starts its rich floral display as early as March. This annual houseplant will give most pleasure if it is placed in a cool, airy, well-lit (but not too sunny) location. Some species do well outdoors.

The **butterfly flower** (*Schizanthus*) blooms in the late spring. It is noted for its unusual flowers, which have divided lobes reminiscent of orchids. If it isn't well cared for the soft foliage becomes a feeding ground for aphids. The plant can do well in a sunny place, but needs plenty of moisture to compensate, plus a little fertiliser every two weeks.

43

The gloxinia family

The **African violet** (*Saint-paulia ionantha*) is by far the best-known of all the Gesneriaceae, or gloxinia family — and with good reason. This little rosette plant provides a continuous floral display in a whole range of colours from white to pink, and takes only a short rest in winter. Coming originally from the forests of

*The flowers of the Cape primrose (*Streptocarpus *hybrids) last for a long time if the plant is kept in a cool, shady place.*

East Africa, the African violet prefers a temperature of not less than 64°F (18°C) throughout the year — but don't allow the air around it to become dry. Because it's a forest plant it won't like direct sunlight or cold, chalky water.

The **Cape primrose** (*Streptocarpus* hybrids) blooms from the end of April through until the autumn. Its flowers may be blue, violet, pink, red or white. Cut off the first flower shoot, as this encourages the plant to grow more vigorously. In a vase the flowers will last longer than a fortnight. Avoid putting the

plant in direct sunlight, and keep it moist and moderately warm.

The **gloxinia** (*Sinningia* hybrids) bears large, bell-shaped

The Cape primrose is quite easy to propagate. Cut off a leaf and put it in a glass of water. The first roots will appear after only a few days. The new plant develops as soon as you have planted the rooting leaf in a pot, and quickly bursts into flower.

flowers with a velvety texture. Their varied colours stand out against the spreading dark-green leaves, which are soft and hairy. This pot plant produces its first flowers towards the end of spring and continues throughout the summer. It needs a half-shaded location with plenty of moisture and fresh air (but no draughts). If well cared for it will grow for several years.

The cheerful **hot water plants** (*Achimenes* hybrids) are easy to grow from their grub-shaped rhizomes. You won't have much trouble persuading them to flower from July right through to September. These plants have no particular soil requirements, but should always be kept in a humid, airy environment.

Hot water plants (Achimenes *hybrids) are easy to look after, and flower from July to September.*

Gloxinias (Sinningia *hybrids) have long been cultivated as houseplants.*

Plants that flower continuously

The **red-hot cat's tail** (*Acalypha*) flowers from April onwards into October. It belongs to the spurge family, and like most of its close cousins it likes a well-lit position away from direct sunlight. It should always be kept warm, and draughts should be avoided at all costs. It often develops a yellow leaf or two, especially if it hasn't been regularly watered. The only solution is to trim off the leaf and resume regular watering — although you should water sparingly from November to January. The more you prune the plant in spring, the more branches it will form. Its drooping tassels of red or white flowers make it an excellent candidate for a hanging basket.

The **zebra plant** (*Aphelandra squarrosa*) is grown not only for its yellow flowers but for the large, decorative green leaves with their contrasting white veins. With a little care and experience, a zebra plant can be persuaded to flower all year round. It needs a well-lit position and (more importantly) a warm environment.

The **rose of China** (*Hibiscus rosa-sinensis*) provides a wonderful floral display in colours of all kinds — red or pink, cream and white through to yellow and orange. The flowers themselves last only a day or two, but their is a continual succession of them.

Some of its varieties have complex flowers, and like other hibiscus plants it will flower well into the autumn. The lush, dark-green foliage is another good reason for including these plants in your collection.

The rose of China particularly enjoys an occasional spraying. It should also be pruned frequently to encourage stronger growth. It manages well in a sunny position, as long as it's well supplied with fertiliser and kept continuously moist. It can also be grown as a potted shrub or a standard.

Madagascar jasmine (*Stephanotis floribunda*) is a highly fragrant plant. It loves a sunny position, but should not be moved about. If it gets plenty of fertiliser from March until the end of August, its white flower clusters will blossom from June to September.

The **wax plant** (*Hoya*) has similarly sweet-smelling flowers, and will grow splendidly if it's trained over a trellis. The plant flowers from May to September. In winter it should be kept a little cooler and watered less. Even in summer it should not be watered too much.

Yesterday, today and tomorrow (*Brunfelsia*) produces magnificent flowers that fade after about three days (hence the name), but can be

*With the right kind of care the rose of China (*Hibiscus rosa-sinensis*) can grow as high as 10 ft (3 m), even under normal room conditions.*

Yesterday, today and tomorrow (Brunfelsia paucifolia *var.* calycina) *produces magnificent flowers that last for an amazingly long time.*

more strongly if you keep it slightly cooler and dryer from November onwards.

Chinese jasmine (*Jasminum polyanthum*) is among the most fragrant of all houseplants. If you train it into a wreath shape, it will produce a continuous display of white, tubular flowers from June to September. Even in the home it is easy to make this plant flower over and over again. Repot regularly, put it in a cool, bright, airy place — and don't forget to water it at regular intervals. If the leaves start to drop, don't worry: there'll soon be new growth to replace them. Chinese jasmine can also be trained into a bushy habit with frequent pruning.

seen almost the whole year through. Its large, shiny leaves form a marvellously decorative backdrop to the deep-blue or violet-coloured flowers. Prune back the long shoots and the plant will become nice and bushy. It should also be repotted after flowering has stopped. It's best to keep the plant in a warm, well-lit place all year round, but it will flower

Common white jasmine (Jasminum officinale) *can fill a whole room with its breathtaking scent. Flowering period: June to September.*

Plants that flower with dormant periods

The **common hydrangea** (*Hydrangea macrophylla*) makes a very impressive houseplant. In a room it prefers a half-shaded position. It also looks its best if it's placed apart from other plants. Hydrangeas will last for many years. When the umbels have finished flowering, they should be removed, together with part of their stems. After repotting, the plant should be left in a shady spot outside. It overwinters best in a well-ventilated place that is pretty much free of frost.

Passion flowers (*Passiflora*) are climbing plants from Central and South America that produce magnificent blooms. The flowers form multicoloured wreaths: some are white, some have blue or violet tints and some are red. The passion

flower needs a warm, well-lit position from spring through to autumn. From the end of May it can even be left outdoors.

Sometimes the young shoots start to develop smaller leaves, or the buds become small and the flowers drop off before they are fully developed. This is usually caused by a shortage of nutrients, and the answer is plenty of fertiliser. Cuttings will root fairly quickly in warm, damp soil. In winter the plants should be kept significantly cooler, and will need less moisture.

The **New Zealand tea** (*Leptospermum scoparium*) looks similar to the myrtle in its leaves and habit. In summer it needs

plenty of watering (preferably with soft water). This will produce excellent, rosy-red blooms from May to June. In winter the plant needs a well-lit, very cool position.

The **glory lily** (*Gloriosa*) is commonly mistaken for an orchid. This is because its flowers (red, or sometimes yellow) are turned upwards rather oddly while the stamens hang down. This plant needs lots of moisture. The rhizomes should be kept dry and moderately warm through the winter, and it's important to avoid damaging them. In March they can be buried in damp soil with the just the tips protruding.

The common hydrangea (Hydrangea macrophylla) is deciduous, and should be kept cool through the winter.

What makes **bougainvillea**
(*Bougainvillea*) remarkable is
its leaf bracts, which are prized
far more than its flowers.
Against such a magnificent
display, the flowers themselves
simply pale into insignificance.
Training a bougainvillea up a
small trellis or into a wreath
shape produces a really
vigorous display of colour,
because the green leaves are no
longer visible among the bracts.

Even if the colours die back,
don't throw the plant away.
Give it a really thorough
pruning and repot it, then leave
it in a well-lit place out of the
sun. It will soon put out new
shoots. In summer, put your
bougainvillea outside in a
bright, sunny position, but
come September move it
indoors to a cool, relatively dry
place. During the main

Left *In winter the passion flower
(Passiflora caerula) needs a cool, dry
position with plenty of light.*

Right *The flowering maple (Abutilon
hybrids) should be moved into a
cool, well-lit position in the late
autumn. Water it only sparingly in
winter.*

flowering period (April to July),
give it a regular weekly feed and
plenty of water. Colours range
from cream, salmon and pink
via red to violet.

Flowering maples (*Abutilon*
hybrids) come in many different
guises. The foliage may be light
green or speckled, while the
flower colours range from
cream through yellow and
orange to dark red. It can flower
throughout the year and grows

into quite an impressive tub
plant.

In summer you needn't worry
about putting a flowering maple
in the garden, but in winter it
will need a cool, well-lit place
indoors. The flowers will
benefit from regular watering
and fertilising from March to
August, and the leaves will also
become thicker. The more you
prune a flowering maple, the
bushier it will become.

Although beautiful and easy to
look after, this plant has certain
disadvantages if you are a
stickler for cleanliness.
However carefully you look
after it, it will lose a leaf or two
every now and then, and the
flowers will drop as they wilt.
But if you're happy to clean up
after it, this needn't put you off
— and the lovely flowers are
ample compensation.

Winter flowers

A pot plant in bloom can provide great deal of pleasure on a dull winter's day, and these days there is a wide selection of winter-flowering plants. As bulbs are induced to sprout ever earlier, so the flowering period can be extended at will. Even so, the majority of houseplants are dormant, at least to some degree, during the cold season.

Cacti, for example, stop growing almost entirely. Other plants respond to the less intense winter light by requiring less water and no food at all — but they do have to be kept cool. Plants in a warm room will continue to develop, and need regular watering if they are not to dry out. Light, water, warmth and nutrients must all be carefully regulated and kept in balance with each other. Too much or too little of any these, and the houseplants will suffer accordingly.

There is one exception to the norm: a group of winter-flowering plants for which the cold season is also the main growing period. Their dormant period is in the summer months, when most of them will be quite happy in the open air. The plants need energy to produce flowers, so they must be watered regularly. If you forget, a thorough soaking in the bath or sink may often be enough to rescue them. In

The florist's cyclamen (Cyclamen persicum) is the traditional winter-flowering plant.

winter, especially, don't water your plants straight from the cold tap: the shock may be too much for any houseplant. Always let the water stand for a while, or else use lukewarm water.

Another very common problem for houseplants in winter is chilly draughts from open windows. Cold air from outside can be very difficult for winter-flowering plants to cope with. Camellias, for example, will invariably respond by dropping their buds, flowers and leaves if they are exposed to sudden changes in temperature. So if you *have* to open a window, make sure you shield your houseplants from the draught. Even a sheet of paper will help.

The **florist's cyclamen** (*Cyclamen persicum*) is easy to look after. This soft, fresh plant provides a great deal of pleasure in winter, when it should be kept in a cool, moist, well-ventilated and well-lit position on a window sill. If the temperature goes above 59°F (15°C), there will be hardly any flowers and the leaves will turn yellow. On the other hand, the cyclamen is also sensitive to frost; if the temperature drops to around freezing the flowers will shrivel.

It is best to water cyclamens from below, i.e. by putting water in the saucer or outer pot in which the plant pot is standing. If you need to water it from above, make sure that no water gets to the centre of the flower or collects on the corm. The best potting mixture is a light, sandy soil with plenty of nutrients. When cyclamens have finished flowering, keep them fed and watered until they start to die back naturally — then stop watering and keep the soil bone dry until new growth starts to appear. If they're properly fed, cyclamens seldom need repotting.

Cyclamens are propagated by sowing from seed. You can even do this successfully indoors: simply sow the seeds in moist garden peat and keep them warm. It's important to cover the seed tray with glass or foil so that the air around the plants is always kept humid.

The **flamingo flower** (*Anthurium-Scherzerianum* hybrids) comes from the tropical forests of Central America, and will flourish as a houseplant. The plant does best in moist, shaded and warm conditions. To ensure it remains healthy, water it daily with boiled water and give it a weekly spraying with lukewarm water. The ideal temperature for it is 68°F (20°C) all year round, and the soil should be well aerated, with plenty of nutrients. Larger plants can be propagated by division.

The flamingo flower (Anthurium–Scherzerianum hybrids) is best suited to the shade — a rare advantage among flowering plants.

Azaleas (*Rhododendron simsii* hybrids) will flower longer if they are kept in a cool place. They should never be allowed to dry out. At the end of May, when the plant has finished flowering, the pot should be put outdoors in the half-shade. But don't just leave it there, because even in summer azaleas require frequent feeding with a lime-free fertiliser. Before bringing the plant indoors, repot it in an acid potting compost (you can buy special composts for azaleas and other ericaceous plants).

Japanese camellias (*Camellia japonica*) are the ornamental equivalent of the tea plant. They come in many varieties, and in all shades from red to white. The flowers themselves vary enormously from small to large and from simple to complex. The prerequisites for good growth and development are regular watering and fertilising, and a place where the plant can stand without having to be moved, especially when it's in bud. Camellias are very sensitive to hard water, so it's best to use rainwater. They need plenty of light, but avoid direct sunlight at all costs, and don't allow them to get too hot.

The **crown of thorns** (*Euphorbia milii*) belongs to the spurge family. It flowers from October through into March, and its small flowers are pink, red, yellow or white. This lovely plant can be placed in direct sunlight, but shouldn't be watered too much. During the

winter water with care, and never allow the plant to become too wet for long periods. The crown of thorns needs repotting only once every two years. The best soil for this purpose is a cactus potting compost enriched with a little loam.

The **poinsettia** (*Euphorbia pulcherrima*) is yet another member of the spurge family. It has brightly coloured leaf

*The poinsettia (*Euphorbia pulcherrima*) may keep its glorious display of coloured bracts until well into May.*

All parts of euphorbias are poisonous, and you should always bear this in mind if you cut or scratch yourself on a crown of thorns. Never allow the sap of the plant to get inside the wound.

bracts, while the flowers themselves are insignificant. Traditionally coloured red, the bracts are also found in several other shades, including pink,

yellow, white and even particoloured (pink and yellow).

The poinsettia should be watered generously from October to February (both before and during the flowering period); then watering should be reduced. Once the bracts start to lose their attractiveness, prune the plant vigorously and put it in a very warm, dry place. It can be repotted in fresh compost when new growth starts to appear, by which time it will need more watering and regular feeds. Prune back the new shoots to encourage more vigorous growth and branching.

Right *The amaryllis (*Hippeastrum hybrids*) with its innumerable different varieties makes a wonderful foil to an arrangement of foliage plants.*

The **flaming Katy** (*Kalanchoe*) has cornered the market for many years. It flowers in a variety of colours. Being a succulent, it won't be too unhappy if you give it less water for a little while. It can also tolerate a sunny position. The plant is propagated by means of cuttings. Left to itself, the flaming Katy is spring-flowering; commercial growers induce it to flower at other times by controlling the amount of light it receives. Make sure the plant gets at least 14 hours of total darkness for a period of six to eight weeks; even a street lamp outside can be enough to stop the flowers forming.

The **amaryllis** (*Hippeastrum*) is noted for its very large flowers. There are innumerable varieties on the market, with colours ranging from snow-white through salmon, orange and pink to dark red, and including some highly variegated forms. These glorious bulb plants will flower from January to April. New or overwintered bulbs should be stored in a warm, well-lit place. When repotting, make sure the neck of the bulb is well clear of the soil, or it can easily rot. Remove any wilted leaves.

Growing from bulbs

Crocuses, tulips, narcissi and hyacinths are attractive early-flowering plants that can be brought into flower while the snow is still lying outside. Choose your time to plant the bulbs according to when you'd like them to bloom — but to ensure flowering over the Christmas period you must buy prepared bulbs, perhaps as early as the beginning of September. These will be clearly labelled by the supplier. If the flowers are earmarked for February, you can plant them later, around November.

Fill your pots or bowls with loose compost, then bury the bulbs and tubers so the tops are just visible. Plant as many as you can in each bowl without allowing the bulbs to touch. Water the soil a little, and leave the bowls in a cool, dark place such as a cellar or garage. If it isn't dark enough there, cover them with black polythene.

Bulbs can be overwintered as late as the early spring, but you will need to store the pots or bowls in leaves or peat to protect them from frost.

If you don't have a garden, cellar or garage where you can leave the bulbs, a balcony may well be enough. Put the bowls in a closed chest full of damp peat — and keep the chest out of the sun.

In late winter or early spring there's nothing to beat the lush beauty of hyacinths grown from bulbs.

Once the bulbs and tubers have been kept cool for the required number of weeks — up to the end of January, say — put them in a cool room for a few days, and then transfer them to a moderately warm living room. After that you should try to keep the plants as moist as possible throughout the sprouting period, either by spraying the shoots daily or by placing a piece of glass or transparent foil over the containers.

Hyacinth bulbs don't actually need to be planted in soil, and will even develop if they are placed over a container of water. You can buy bulb glasses (or their plastic equivalents) designed specifically for this purpose. The glass should be filled with water up to about one-tenth of an inch (2 mm) below the bottom of the bulb. On no account let the bulb come into contact with the water. The water level should not be allowed to drop too far, either, so keep it topped up regularly. Once again, the glass with the hyacinth bulb inside it should be kept for several weeks in a cool, dark place. Once the roots are properly developed, and the shoot has grown to just over 2 inches (about 6 cm), the glass can be transferred to a warmer room. At first the bulb will need to be protected from too much light using a little paper cover of some kind. This can be removed

Crocuses, winter aconites and snowdrops are the very first of the spring flowers to appear. All of them can easily be raised indoors if they are planted after the first frosts.

as soon as the flowering shoot begins to push it up.

When the plant has finished flowering, plant the bulbs or tubers in the garden. As soon as the foliage turns yellow, cut it off (so that the bulb can ripen) and apply a little fertiliser.

55

Indoor trees

These large green plants can bring life to the barest of rooms.

The **Norfolk Island pine** (*Araucaria heterophylla*) is one of the most decorative of trees. Its branches grow out radially from a slender trunk to give the plant a lively, elegant shape. Both trunk and branches are covered with thin, light-green needles. The tree is at its most attractive when it has grown to a height of more than 3 ft (90 cm). The Norfolk Island pine requires cool temperatures and plenty of light, and should be watered only sparingly.

Schefflera grows very fast (which makes it ideal for filling an empty corner) but is also very demanding. It doesn't like direct sunlight, and a monthly dose of fertiliser is advisable throughout the summer. The yellow-variegated form is also rather more sensitive. If the temperature falls the leaves often drop, although they will quickly grow again. Be sure to protect it from draughts when airing the room in winter.

The **rubber plant** (*Ficus elastica*) with its many types and varieties is one of the most forgiving of all ornamental trees. It can get used to almost any position, though it doesn't like intense sunlight. It also reacts to stagnant wet conditions by dropping its leaves, so it isn't advisable to water it until the soil surface is properly dry. The rubber plant likes a potting mixture with plenty of nutrients.

The **weeping fig** (*Ficus benjamina*) belongs to the same family as the rubber plant, but is has very different needs. It requires warmth, good light and a watering programme that avoids excessively wet conditions. The white-variegated forms are more sensitive than the green ones, and should not be exposed to sudden drops in temperature. The weeping fig, with its gently drooping branches and small, shiny leaves, makes a highly attractive houseplant that is very easy to look after. If the plant dries out and the leaves fall off, don't throw it away — they'll soon grow back again.

*The weeping fig (*Ficus benjamina*) comes in a number of white-variegated cultivars such as 'Hawaii' and 'Starlight'.*

*The Norfolk Island pine (*Araucaria heterophylla*) needs to stand alone for its beauty to be fully appreciated.*

In contrast to the larger-leaved rubber plant — now rather passé — the weeping fig has recently become very fashionable. Perhaps that's because this plant never loses its grace, no matter how tall and impressive it grows. Even so, it really needs to stand alone for its beauty to be appreciated. The weeping fig can also be trained to form a standard, or even a standard with a spiral trunk.

The **wind flower** or **house lime** (*Sparmannia africana*) is a tree-like shrub with magnificent light-green leaves. Unlike most other indoor trees, it also bears flowers; the white clusters appear in the early spring. Wind flower manages well in centrally heated rooms, but is very sensitive to smoke, gas and exhaust fumes. In winter you can keep the plant cooler, but don't water it as generously as you would in summer — and remember it can't tolerate intense sunlight.

The **Swiss cheese plant** (*Monstera deliciosa*) comes from tropical rain forests, where the large holes or windows in its leaves allow light and rain to reach the lower parts of the plant. Even in living-room conditions, *Monstera* will grow into a tall plant with luxuriant foliage. The enormous leaves, with their highly distinctive design, will give the room a special atmosphere of its own.

The slim, partially woody stem and branches throw out long aerial roots. Don't cut these off. If you guide them back into the soil, they'll turn into feeding roots, enabling the plant to take in more moisture and nutrients. Put the Swiss cheese plant in a nutrient-rich potting compost and always give it plenty of water. Wipe the leaves at frequent intervals. This plant thrives best at a temperature of about 68°F (20°C). It needs plenty of light, but keep it out of direct sunlight.

A Swiss cheese plant should develop holes in its leaves. If it doesn't, your chosen site may be too dark, or the air may be too dry. Move it to a brighter spot and give it a daily spraying.

57

The pleasure of palms

Palm trees are as much at home by the sea as in dense rain forests or on mountain heights. They are among the most beautiful of tropical plants, and are characteristic of the vegetation around the tropics of Cancer and Capricorn.

Palms can generally be counted among the more robust houseplants. Even so, if you want to look after them properly there are several essential things to remember.

Given where palms come from, most people are surprised to learn that only a very few of them can tolerate direct sunlight. This is because palms that are kept indoors will always remain at an immature stage of development. In the wild, they normally grow up in the shade of older, much larger specimens. That's why house palms need a well-lit position that is also protected from direct sunlight. It's always very risky to put palms out into the spring sunshine at the end of a dreary winter — they invariably get sun-scorched. Always start by putting them in the shade of a few trees. In any case, palms don't like it too hot, and most will flourish at temperatures of 64-68°F (18-20°C).

The **parlour palm** (*Chamae-dorea elegans*) grows into a loose bush made up of fronds. In the home it will always remain small and delicate, but it's one of the few palms that will flower easily in room conditions.

The parlour palm, like the many other *Chamaedorea* species, comes from the mountain forests of Central and South America. All forms of *Chamaedorea* prefer a shady position, and will even flourish in a north-facing room; never expose them to direct sunlight. In winter they should be given less water and kept a little cooler — at around 54-59°F (12-15°C). Give them regular weekly doses of fertiliser throughout the summer, and an occasional spraying as a welcome treat. Parlour palms also do really well under a hydroponic regime.

The **betel nut palm** (*Areca catechu*) is a feather palm with elegant deep-green fronds. Its lancet-shaped leaflets stand out in comb-like rows to form fronds that look like feathers. The betel nut palm is at home in tropical Asia, the East Indies and Australia, where it grows to over 65 ft (20 m) in height.

This palm needs plenty of water and plenty of warmth. The temperature must never go below 59°F (15°C), and the surrounding air should always be humid. The pot should stand permanently in a saucer or tray full of water. It's another plant that doesn't enjoy standing in direct sunlight.

Betel nut palms can be propagated from seed. However, the seeds will not germinate until some eight weeks have passed, and only then if the soil has been kept warm and moist, and at an even temperature.

The **Canary Islands date palm** (*Phoenix canariensis*) has fronds lined with long, upturned lancet-shaped leaflets. It's a robust plant that does well in room conditions and will even flourish in a centrally heated environment. In winter it will benefit from cooler, dryer conditions. It can stand in the open air throughout the summer, as long as it's shielded from direct sunlight. This date palm is very easy to propagate from seed; the stones take eight weeks to germinate.

The **golden feather palm** (*Areca lutescens*) is a feather palm that grows in clusters, with several plants growing out of a single rhizome. Each has a slender stem crowned with a large shock of finely divided arching fronds. This handsome plant originally came from Madagascar and the surrounding islands.

*Palms are among the most elegant of all plants. To the left of the picture is a kentia palm (*Howeia forsteriana), and to the right a coconut palm (Cocos nucifera), which has a regrettably short life as an indoor plant.*

The Canary Islands date palm (Phoenix canariensis) *can easily be grown from seed at home.*

The golden feather palm prefers a half-shaded position in the room. The temperature must not drop below 59°F (15°C) for any length of time. The root ball needs to be moist all the time, so keep the pot in a saucer or tray full of water. With its delicate golden tints, this feather palm provides a delightful foil to other plants. Side shoots can be divided and potted separately.

The **windmill palm** (*Trachycarpus fortunei*), found mainly in Asia, has shiny dark-green leaves that radiate from the stem to form massive fan shapes. Around the Mediterranean and on the southern slopes of the Alps it grows out in the open all year round. In fact it's a very hardy plant. As well as being insensitive to cold, it can easily survive short periods of drought.

In winter this palm should be kept cool at around 50°F (10°C); it doesn't care for overheated rooms. It can be propagated from seed, although the seeds will take a month or two to germinate.

The **kentia palm** (*Howeia forsteriana*) is a very large yet elegant palm, with gently arching fronds divided into broad leaflets. It is highly decorative and demands a position on its own.

In most other ways this palm is extremely *un*demanding — it can even tolerate dry, centrally heated air. However, it does need shade. It should never be exposed to direct sunlight, and it isn't suited to outdoor conditions. Every ten days it should be fed with fertiliser.

The **petticoat palm** (*Washingtonia filifera*) from the American continent is one of the fastest-growing palms, but it's also rather sensitive. Keep the root ball moist at all times, and make sure the air around the plant is always extremely humid. If the broad leaves turn yellow, the plant probably needs better lighting conditions. *Washingtonia* is easy to grow from seed; the seedlings appear after four weeks.

The **dwarf fan palm** (*Chamaerops humilis*) is a typical fan palm, and retains a short, stocky habit. It is one of a small group of palms that will survive outdoors throughout the winter in mild climates.

This plant is remarkably easy to look after. It does particularly well if it is kept out in the open from May through to October in a well-lit, airy position. It needs plenty of watering in summer; regular doses of fertiliser (every two or three weeks) are recommended.

The dwarf fan palm can be propagated by removing suckers that rise from the roots and potting them individually in small pots.

Palms that grow in clusters should not be replanted in separate pots. They will rarely survive such treatment, preferring to live in close proximity to one another. They can be replanted every three years, but even then they should always be kept together.

The parlour palm (Chamaedorea elegans) will flower very quickly if it is looked after properly.

Palm-like plants

Many attractive houseplants are often mistaken for palms, either because they look like palms or because the word 'palm' appears somewhere in their name. From a botanical point of view, none of these plants are palms. Nonetheless, they share the same austere beauty and clearly defined structure — and like most palms they have a long stem crowned with a shock of narrow leaves.

These palm-like plants include the dragon tree (*Dracaena*), papyrus (*Cyperus*), *Pachypodium geayi*, cast iron plant (*Aspidistra elatior*), palm lily (*Yucca*) and various *Schefflera* species, to name but a few. Although they aren't actually palms, they are popular for similar reasons. Their elegant shapes blend well with the stark surroundings of a really modern living room. But to see them at their best, you should position them on their own against a pale, relatively plain background.

True palms all have very similar requirements. The species described here come from every part of the world, and are thus very adaptable to different forms of treatment. This can be an advantage in the home, where conditions are often so variable.

Most plants don't look very attractive when they lose their bottom leaves, but the same cannot be said for the **dragon tree** (*Dracaena*). This imposing plant is often at its most elegant when a single large cluster of fronds is left at the top of its highly attractive stem. If, on the other hand, you prefer a shorter habit, just cut off the top at a height of about 5 ft (1.5 m).

Not quite as attractive as palms: (from left to right) Schefflera arboricola *and various dragon trees:* Dracaena marginata 'Tricolor' *and* D. marginata.

This will encourage the side stems and give the plant a marvellously exotic feel.

The dragon tree proper comes from the Canary Islands, while the many other *Dracaena* species are scattered across the tropics of Africa and Asia. They belong to the agave family. All of them need plenty of light but cannot tolerate intense sunlight; morning or evening sun suits them better. If the variegated species don't get the light they need, they will revert to their original green.

If dragon trees are kept in a warm spot all year round, they will always need plenty of watering. You can, however, keep them cooler in winter as long as the ambient temperature is above 55°F (13°C) — in which case you should give them less water during this period. During the main growth period (May to August), you should give them a regular weekly feed with a good general houseplant fertiliser to encourage the development of variegated colours.

The **papyrus plant** and its close relatives (*Cyperus*) are a very different kettle of fish. Their decorative leaves fan out from a long, thin stem to create an umbrella shape. (One of them is known as the umbrella plant.) They belong to the reed family, and are at home in marshes and along riverbanks throughout the tropics.

The papyrus is a popular houseplant. It's relatively easy to

*The aspidistra or cast iron plant (*Aspidistra elatior*) readily adapts to any home environment.*

care for, and somehow manages to look lush and graceful at the same time. Keep the pot permanently in a bowl or tray full of water. Never let it dry out, or the leaf tips will turn yellow. In summer you can plant it in a small garden pond. If, despite your efforts, the plant suffers from dryness, the best solution is a thorough pruning. Add some fertiliser to the water every two weeks.

Papyrus is quite easy to propagate from a stem cutting, but there's a special way of doing it. Cut off the tips of the leaves and put the cutting upside down in a glass of water. This is because the germination point is at the base of the leaves. You should see the first roots appearing within a few days.

Pachypodium lamerii is superficially palm-like in appearance. In fact it's a succulent plant belonging to the periwinkle family, which also includes the oleander. It has a thick, spiky stem crowned with a round shock of long, leathery, dark-green leaves. This attractive plant comes from the dry steppe and semidesert regions of southern Africa. It needs plenty of light, but doesn't seem to worry if it isn't watered very much.

The **aspidistra** or **cast iron plant** (*Aspidistra elatior*) is, despite all appearances, a member of the lily family. In the 19th century it was an extremely popular houseplant, especially among the poorer classes. This was probably because it was so sturdy and tolerant. The aspidistra will grow quite happily even in a dark room.

Plants with attractive leaves

Many plants are cultivated because of the bright colours and patterns on their leaves. With plants like these it's often tempting to grow too many different kinds together, which can make the resulting display look rather crowded. It's better to choose just a few closely related species. Besides looking more attractive, the bright colours will give your room a visual focus.

Few plants can rival the variety of leaf colours and patterns offered by the **begonias** (*Begonia* hybrids). The hybrids of the fan begonia (*B. rex*) are especially colourful; they form rhizomes and like a well-lit but not too sunny position. Leaf begonias such as *B. metallica* or *B. corallina* hybrids prefer half-shade, and temperatures around 68°F (20°C).

In winter you should keep begonias at a minimum of 59-64°F (15-18°C). During this period they become dormant and rather unattractive. Come the spring, though, you can repot them in a fresh, light compost — and they'll immediately put out new shoots in response.

The **flame nettle** (*Coleus-Blumei* hybrids) comes in an

Undemanding yet conspicuous — the flame nettle (Coleus–Blumei hybrids)

infinite variety of colours ranging from red to green through a series of yellowy tints. This plant needs very little care, and can be left outside in summer, but in winter warm conditions are essential. Stem cuttings will take root without any difficulty. Prune the flame nettle frequently if you want it to form a bushy habit.

The **nerve plant** (*Fittonia verschaffeltii*) probably takes its name from the complex herringbone pattern formed by its leaf veins. These are either red or silver depending on the subspecies. This plant needs a lot of care and attention: it can easily be killed by a cool, damp atmosphere. Cold water on the leaves can be just as bad, and it doesn't care for direct sunlight.

The nerve plant does well in a glass tank, a heated winter garden or an enclosed window display.

The **prayer plant** (*Maranta leuconeura*) is a remarkably pretty house plant. Its leaves are usually olive green splashed with light green, and with strikingly red veins. It will grow well if kept warm, but it's extremely sensitive to sunlight — and the air around it must be kept very humid. It's much easier to look after this plant if you keep it in a glass tank or a large goldfish bowl.

Angel's wings (*Caladium-Bicolor* hybrids) is the name of a foliage plant with tuber-like roots. The leaves are boldly coloured with reds, yellows, pinks and sometimes whites on a green background. This plant, too, is decidely sensitive, preferring an extremely humid environment that is protected from draughts.

In autumn the leaves wither and lose their attractiveness. Your best plan is simply to overwinter the tubers in dry sand at a temperature of around 64°F (18°C). Take them out in March, plant them in fresh, finely divided soil and put the pot in a warm, humid spot. Give them plenty of water throughout the spring and summer, but gradually reduce the amounts as the growing season comes to a close.

The **croton** or **Joseph's coat** (*Codiaeum variegatum*) is quite remarkable for the colour, variety and brilliance of its foliage. As a shrub it's well suited to a home environment. It needs a well-lit position that is protected from direct sunlight. Never let the temperature drop below 64°F (18°C) at any time of the year.

These brightly patterned leaves make prayer plants particularly beautiful, but they need plenty of warmth and humidity. This is the magnificent cultivar Maranta leuconeura *'Massangeana'.*

65

Plants with fragrant foliage

Flowers give off their scent spontaneously. Leaves must normally be touched or rubbed for their fragrance to come out. However, with some foliage plants one strong draught from a window can be enough to make you suddenly aware of the scent from their leaves. It's caused by the evaporation of the essential oils that are stored there.

Eucalypts or **gums** (*Eucalyptus*) with their attractive blue-green foliage need plenty of light and air. Apart from this they are no problem to look after, and you can even put them outside in the summer. Make sure to give them a weekly dose of fertiliser during the summer months.

The **sweet bay** (*Laurus nobilis*) has probably been cultivated longer than any other plant of this type. Its decorative qualities have been acknowledged and appreciated for centuries. The dark-green colouring is particularly effective in a kitchen window. The sweet bay also makes one of the

Rosemary (Rosmarinus officinalis) grows better if you put it outside for the summer.

most attractive tub plants. It can be pruned so that it grows into a pyramid shape, and will even work well as a standard. This plant will tolerate direct sunlight as long as you give it plenty of water at the same time. It thrives on a sandy potting compost with plenty of lime.

Scented geraniums (*Pelargonium*) will grow into attractive bushes if they are pruned frequently. Their flowers are rather insignificant compared with the magnificent blooms produced by their close relatives, the flowering pelargoniums. Scented geraniums more than make up for this with their leaves, which in some species are beautiful as well as highly fragrant. Their scents range from camphor to apple and lemon.

These plants, too, are very easy to care for. In summer they prefer a warm, sunny position, and can also be left out in the open. Never allow the root ball to stay dry for any length of time or the leaves will start to turn yellow.

Scented geraniums are quite simple to propagate. Take a stem cutting with just one pair of leaves and plant it in wet soil. The cutting will take root after only a few days. Use a compost with plenty of nutrients and a high sand content.

Swedish ivy (*Plectranthus*) is a member of the mint family, and its lemony scent is supposed to repel moths. It's a highly adaptable plant that

*This eucalypt (*Eucalyptus gunnii*) rarely flowers — but when it does it's a sight for sore eyes.*

flourishes in the sun as well as in the half-shade. It also copes very well with irregular watering, and with variable temperature and humidity levels. In winter it's happy even at 50°F (10°C) provided you give it less water. It likes an ordinary light compost. The leaf shoots can be used for propagation at any time during the summer. They will root quickly in a light, moist potting mixture.

Rosemary (*Rosmarinus officinalis*) is a delightful evergreen shrub, much prized for its herbal properties. The leaves have a camphor-like scent and taste very slightly

bitter. In summer, rosemary produces a lovely display of small, bluish-white flowers.

The plant is fairly easy to look after. It needs a sunny position and should not be kept too moist. If you leave it outside during the summer, it will become much stronger to face the winter.

Luxuriant ferns

Ferns may have no flowers, but they more than make up for this with their lush, green fronds lined with beautifully formed leaflets. Some people think they're difficult to look after, but they needn't be if you follow two or three simple rules.

First, never put a fern in the sun; it much prefers the shade. Second, never let a fern dry out. If it does, the only solution is a radical pruning followed by a really good soaking: leave the pot in a large container of water until the fronds are completely green again. Third, always keep your ferns at a warm, even temperature. A few species can cope with a cooler environment, but all of them are sensitive to sudden changes of temperature.

Follow all these rules, treat your ferns to a regular weekly spraying, and they'll give you nothing but pleasure. Ferns are particularly suitable for a

*These ferns make an attractive group — **left**: Davallia bullata; **right** (top to bottom): ladder fern (Nephrolepis cordifolia), maidenhair fern (Adiantum raddianum), sword fern (Nephrolepis exaltata), ball fern (Davallia mariesii) and Davallia solida.*

bathroom, where the dampness provides just the kind of atmosphere their deep-green fronds require.

The **maidenhair fern** (*Adiantum raddianum*) is well known for its grace and beauty. It needs a half-shaded position and a temperature of at least 61°F (16°C). It's just as important to water it regularly and feed it every two or three weeks during the summer. The best fertiliser for this purpose is the ordinary liquid feed sold for all green plants — but use a weaker concentration than the packet suggests. Maidenhair ferns are ideal for glass tanks and enclosed window displays.

Leather fern (*Arachniodes*) is the name given to a dark-green fern with thick, leathery, often brownish-coloured fronds. The fronds are triangular in shape and tripinnate in form, and often grow to over 3 ft (up to 1 m) in length. This fern also likes cooler temperatures — 59°F (15°C) is quite enough. Use a good indoor plant fertiliser. The leather fern grows extremely well in a half-shaded position.

The **bird's nest fern** (*Asplenium nidus*) comes from deep in the tropical rain forests, where it lives as an epiphyte, growing on the branches of trees. The long fronds are undivided and therefore not very fern-like apart from their deep-green colouring. Together they form a broad, spreading funnel or 'nest' which channels rainwater downward. It is hardly surprising, then, that

watering this unusual plant from above produces excellent results. In fact it should be sprayed every day. The bird's nest fern grows into a magnificent plant in the shade of other, larger plants.

The **sword fern** (*Nephrolepis exaltata*) is one of the most popular ferns to be found in the home. To flourish properly it needs a relatively shady position with plenty of humidity and temperatures above 64°F (18°C). If it's in a centrally heated room, humidifiers are essential to create the necessary conditions.

The **stag's horn fern** (*Platycerium*) is yet another much sought-after fern. There are some seventeen species, all of which live as epiphytes in the high canopies of the world's tropical rain forests. They make excellent plants for hanging baskets.

The stag's horn fern ideally requires shade and plenty of humidity, though it will also grow in dry conditions. The temperature should be around 64-68°F (18-20°C). Never try to clean the fronds: you risk damaging the down-like surface.

The bird's nest fern (Asplenium nidus) needs a very humid environment.

A hanging garden indoors

It may be that you don't have enough room for plants on your window-sill. If so, a few hanging plants may well provide the answer, even indoors. You can suspend the pot or basket from the ceiling or in a suitable window bay. In many ways a hanging plant is just like a climbing plant. The only

difference is that shoots are allowed to hang down rather than being encouraged to climb.

Hanging plants can be particularly effective on a shelf or a cupboard. Their trailing greenery helps to soften the straight, horizontal lines of the furniture. Plants growing down from a pot perched on a column (in the

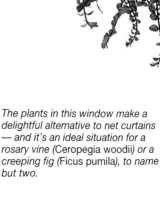

The plants in this window make a delightful alternative to net curtains — and it's an ideal situation for a rosary vine (Ceropegia woodii) *or a creeping fig* (Ficus pumila), *to name but two.*

From left to right: a Columnea hybrid, a wax plant (Hoya), a sweetheart plant (Philodendron scandens) and a burro's tail cactus (Sedum morganianum).

corner of a room, for example) can also make a very attractive display. But you should always make sure that there is enough light for the plants.

The shoots from some plants — mind your own business, for example — won't hang more than 4-8 in (10-20 cm) below the edge of the pot. If you put them in a pot or basket hanging from the ceiling, use a long chain to bring the plant down to eye level.

With hanging plants you must ensure the pot is really stable. If it isn't, the overhanging shoots may eventually tip it over. And do remember that the air in a room is warmer near the ceiling, so plants at this height are going to need more watering. In practice it's all too easy to give them less water, because you don't notice them during your regular rounds with the watering can. The best precaution is to buy a good-sized pot. The larger the pot, the more stable it is and the

71

more water it can accommodate in the soil.

When using a hanging basket, remember to put your plant pot on a saucer to stop water dripping down. Better still, make sure you get a saucer for the pot when you're buying the plant.

The green, heart-shaped leaves of the **creeping fig** (*Ficus pumila*) look particularly attractive when they're hanging down between an assortment of other plants. Like all *Ficus* species the creeping fig needs plenty of light, but doesn't like direct sunlight. This plant must never be allowed to dry out, but don't keep it too wet, either.

The **rosary vine** (*Ceropegia woodii*) makes a fresh, lively display for a hanging basket at eye level. Children, especially, will love them. This plant is really no problem to look after, and thrives equally well in the sun or half-shade. Like other *Ceropegia* species it is to some extent succulent (as witness the small, fleshy leaves), so you won't need to water it as much as your other hanging plants. The rosary vine is extremely easy to propagate from its tiny tubers. Just plant them in soil, keep them warm and moist, and they will very quickly take root.

Tradescantias or **spiderworts** (*Tradescantia*) are an extremely popular group of plants. They include some beautiful foliage species that grow quickly to form a glorious hanging display.

All forms of spiderwort will propagate very easily from stem cuttings. You should plant about five or six cuttings at a time in a pot full of damp soil. Tradescantias with a lot of white in their leaves need plenty of light but don't like intense sunlight. Darker-leaved forms prefer the half-shade.

There are many species and varieties of **Columnea**, some with luxuriant floral displays. It's hardly surprising that they

Left *The Italian bellflower variety Campanula isophylla 'Alba' can even cope with hard, chalky water.*

Right *The sword fern (*Nephrolepis exaltata*) is the ideal hanging plant for a shady location.*

have long been popular as houseplants. They grow well in the home, and their cascading flowers make them the ideal choice for a hanging basket. After flowering it's advisable to prune out any untidy growth so the plants form a neater shape. The form with variegated foliage is particularly attractive, though it bears fewer flowers.

The **Italian bellflower** (*Campanula isophylla*) is another plant that thrives in the home. The stems don't hang down very far, so be sure to bring the hanging basket down to eye level. The flowers are lilac-blue or sometimes white, and grow in dense profusion, bringing a real splash of brightness into the room.

Bellflowers will bloom just as well in a north-facing window as in a south-facing one, where you'll also need to protect them from the midday sun. Keep them a little cooler and dryer in the winter, and cut back the shoots to within an inch or two (a few centimetres). As soon as the new shoots have become established, repot your bell-flower in fresh potting compost, and keep it warmer and moister again.

The **spider plant** (*Chlorophytum comosum*) makes an ideal hanging plant. It has long, grass-like leaves, and throws out long shoots with plantlets at the end. The spider plant is relatively tolerant, adapting quickly to sudden changes in conditions. It will even grow in a cool, poorly lit situation —

The hanging fig variety Ficus radicans 'Variegata' *needs plenty of light, though direct sunlight isn't advisable.*

above a staircase, for instance. Even so, it flourishes most readily when it's given plenty of warmth and light but no direct sunlight.

Grape ivy (*Rhoicissus rhomboidea*) is the ideal plant for a shady room. This indoor vine even likes a bathroom, where it will grow in profusion. It's fairly insensitive to temperature changes, and won't be too upset if you forget to water it now and again.

The true **ivies** (*Hedera*) are similarly suited to the shade, but need to be kept moist at all times. Species or varieties of ivy with light-coloured variegated leaves can even cope in a sunny position.

If you keep ivy (*Hedera*) too warm in winter, it will become thin and drawn, and will tend to shed its leaves.

A touch of the exotic

Among the more exotic houseplants are the **bromeliads**. This is the general name given to all the members of the pineapple family. Bromeliads form a very large and disparate group of plants, restricted (in the wild) to tropical and subtropical regions of the American continent. The group includes some 45 species that are grown and propagated by gardeners. Among the best-known of these are the magnificent silvery-grey urn plant and the pretty little earth stars (*Cryptanthus*), as well as *Billbergia* and the various tillandsias.

It was Christopher Columbus who brought the first news of the **pineapple** (*Ananas comosus*) to Europe in 1493. He'd discovered the plant on his second voyage to the West Indies. The pineapple was probably introduced to European greenhouses around 1690, and its delicious fruit soon made it a valuable and much sought-after plant.

The **tillandsias** (*Tillandsia*) are a fascinating group of bromeliads, and they can easily be bought over the counter at most garden shops. They're very tolerant plants: in their native habitat they can flourish on little more than the moisture in the atmosphere. Even so, you'd be well advised to buy them only from a specialist outlet. Tillandsias prefer warmth and high humidity. So spray them spray them several times a day.

The bromeliads can broadly be divided into two groups: **terrestrial** species that normally grow in the soil, and **epiphytes**. The latter are so-called because in the wild they grow on trees, especially in moss patches where branches divide.

Most bromeliads have their leaves arranged in rosettes. At the centre of each rosette is a tube or bowl that in many plants forms a natural reservoir for rainwater. It also forms a trap for leaves and small animals, which gradually decompose to form a highly nutritious 'soup'. You can easily replicate this process at home by pouring water and liquid fertiliser into the centre of the leaf rosette as well as the soil.

Different bromeliads require different levels of light and temperature, but there's a useful rule of thumb that applies to them all. Plants with hard,

Bromeliads normally take several years to flower. However, mature plants that are reluctant to produce flowers can be given a little encouragement. Place the plant and an apple in a sealed polythene bag: the ethylene gas given off by the apple will induce the plant to flower more readily.

silvery-grey leaves need plenty of light and relatively cool temperatures — around 59°F (15°C). If, on the other hand, the leaves are soft (and particularly if they are green as well), the plant will need a rather warmer, shadier position at about 68°F (20°C). On warm summer days, most bromeliads respond well to a spell in the open air — and there's nothing to beat a shower of warm rain. If you plant them out in a window box, or in a stone trough on a patio, they make a highly individual display.

Bromeliads don't like excessively wet soil, which can easily cause the roots to rot. In their natural habitat they're accustomed to drying out, but plants that form a natural watertight 'vase' with their overlapping leaves should have the 'vase' filled at all times.

Bromeliads usually flower only once, but the flower lasts for a long time. During the flowering period the plant forms offsets that can be used for propagation. Remove the offset with a sharp knife, leave it in the open air for a day to dry out, and pot it in a light, moist compost that is open and well drained.

Don't be too disappointed if your bromeliads fail to flower straight away. The leaves are decorative on their own, and their attractive habit goes nicely with taller, bushier houseplants.

The urn plant (Aechmea fasciata) has a gorgeous display of pink bracts. It's also tolerant of dry, centrally heated air.

Spines galore

Cacti have spines and roses have thorns — that's the usual distinction. Botanically speaking, though, the distinction is between spines and prickles. Spines consist of modified twigs, leaves or even roots, and are part of the plant's growing tissue. You can't remove a spine from a cactus without damaging it. Rose thorns are no more than prickles, forming part of the plant's outer surface. Since they aren't bound to the underlying tissue, they can easily be removed.

You can fit a lot of cacti into a small space. A window-sill, for instance, is usually enough. If you need more space, you can build a window shelf above it. This is an excellent spot for small cacti, as long as you don't have to open the window very often.

If you're really serious about growing cacti, you're probably going to need:
- small earthenware or plastic pots for repotting
- flat dishes for sowing
- a sheet of glass to lay over them
- a pair of tweezers for pricking out
- small pieces of wood (e.g. old pencils) for pricking out
- adhesive or candle wax for removing spines
- a sharp knife for grafting or taking cuttings
- rubber bands for grafting

- a suitable watering can
- a small magnifying glass to identify pests and diseases
- liquid cactus fertiliser to be used in summer (May–August.

Cacti like a sandy potting mixture, a sunny position and less water than other house-plants. In summer you can cheerfully put them out in the open air. Be careful where you put cacti in winter, because this is vital to the development of flowers. During the winter cacti

need a cool, light and airy location with modest temperature. It's also essential to ensure that from early October until early March the following year they are given now water whatsoever, unless the plants are in very tiny pots where the soil dries out excessively.

Left *Early in the summer a cactus collection can look just like a miniature flower garden.*
Above *The golden barrel cactus* (Echinocactus grusonii)*, with its bright-yellow spines, creates an impressive display.*

Complete winter rest promotes flower production in spring.

Once you get the cactus bug, you'll quickly become a collector. To get you started, though, let's take a look at the main groups of cacti that are suitable for beginners.

The **prickly pears** (*Opuntia*) are so called because most of them produce pleasant, sweet-tasting fruit when they grow in their natural habitat. You can usually identify them by their distinctively jointed, branching stems, made up of broad, flat, swollen pads.

Some species can survive our winters out of doors, and will even grow and flower in the garden. Indeed, most prickly pears are relatively hardy and easy to care for. As houseplants, however, they rarely produce flowers because they don't get enough light. They also rot easily if you overwater them.

Opuntia robusta and Indian fig (*Opuntia ficus-indica*) have

*This Easter cactus (*Rhipsalidopsis*) produces magnificent flowers if it's encouraged to remain dormant during the winter.*

quite large pads. Those of the bunny ears (*Opuntia micro-dasys*) always remain small. This cactus is very pretty, but the tiny, awkwardly hooked spines make it more vicious than the name would suggest.

The *Brasiliopuntia*, from South America, form a very attractive subgroup. They include some species with thinner, more leaf-like branches armed with long, brownish spines.

Columnar cacti are those that grow to form a long stem. Most stand upright, like a column. Few of them flower indoors.

Some columnar cacti are covered with a dense hairy growth. The old man cactus (*Cephalocereus senilis*), for example, has so much white, frizzy hair that you can wash it if it gets too dusty! Treat it like your own hair: lather it up with a little shampoo, then rinse it off and dry it with a hair dryer.

Cleistocactus straussii looks very like the old man cactus, but is covered in dense white bristles rather than hairs. After a few years this plant will grow into a handsome column.

Some columnar species have a strongly ribbed stem with relatively few spines. A good example of this is *Cereus peruvianus*, which has five to eight ribs, each of them armed with sharp spines. Older plants may come into flower, producing large blooms.

Myrtle cacti (*Myrtillocactus*) are easy to look after. Their name comes from the myrtle-like berries they produce in their native habitat. Even the taste is similar to myrtle.

Some cacti have adopted a long, trailing habit like a snake, but in other respects they are much the same as columnar cacti. The long stems are often ribbed. Perhaps the best-known of these cacti is the queen of the night (*Selenicereus grandi-florus*). It produces enormous yellow-and-white flowers that bloom late on a summer evening but wilt before daybreak. You can expect your first flower some five years after sowing.

The queen of the night produces sweet-smelling flowers. Those of its close relative the princess of the night (*Seleni-cereus pteranthus*) are equally magnificent but have no scent.

Strictly speaking, **leaf cacti** are wrongly named — they don't *have* leaves as such. However, their branching stems have become jointed and swollen, giving the appearance of long lines of leaves. Most of these cacti have no spines. There are many species, and all of them produce flowers in great profusion.

The Easter cactus (*Rhipsalidopsis gaertneri*) flowers in the spring, creating a gorgeous display of pink, red or violet blooms. The Christmas cactus (*Schlumbergera truncata*) is very similar, but flowers during the winter. Its gently arching stems bear an equally magnificent floral display that varies in colour from red, white and pink to violet.

Ball or **barrel cacti** are spherical or globular in form. Many have a magnificent array of spines, which is often so colourful that they're worth having even without the flowers. A great number of them will produce flowers from the tiniest of balls, including the *Parodia* and *Rebutia* species. *Eriocactus leninghausii* is bright yellow, and has yellowy-orange flowers as well.

One of the most beautiful cacti in this group is the golden barrel cactus (*Echinocactus grusonii*), which has a deep-green body covered with serried ranks of indestructible bright-yellow or white spines. You can expect to wait some 25 years for it to flower, and then only if it has been standing outside during the summer.

The gently flowering **nipple cacti** are best represented by the *Mammilaria* group (the name actually means 'nipple'). Even when they're very young, these plants will produce lovely wreaths of flowers around the top of the 'nipple'. Some species form large cushions of dense hairy material, and need great care with watering.

Extreme cleanliness is vital for grafting. The freshly cut scion (Gymnocalicium mihanovicii var. rubra) is placed on the freshly cut grafting stock (Cereus peruvianus) and secured with a rubber band.

Other succulents

Succulents are living proof of the remarkable ways in which plants can adapt to harsh climates and unproductive soils. They are at home in deserts, semideserts and other arid regions of the world.

The majority of succulents are known as **leaf succulents**, because they have thick, fleshy leaves that can store large amounts of water. However, many of them, including cacti, are stem succulents, with a swollen stem that acts as a water reservoir. Most of the leaf succulents have a much looser decorative structure than the **stem succulents**. As such they provide a welcome foil to the compact shapes of cacti, making them an essential ingredient of a cactus garden.

Succulents in general need less moisture and fewer soil

Mesembryanthemums must tand in full sunlight if their soft flowers are to open at all.

Even the tiniest of living stones (Lithops) can burst into flower. Their pastel-coloured blooms always come as a surprise.

nutrients than most other plants. They should also be repotted less often than most other plants.

Aloe variegata is a leaf succulent belonging to the lily family. It comes originally from South Africa. It throws out many suckers, which you can separate from the parent plant when they are just under an inch (2 cm) in length. Older plants will flower in January, producing beautiful, brightly coloured tubular flowers.

This plant prefers to stand outside in the summer. When watering, take care that no water goes between the leaves: rot can very easily set in here. Aloe variegata likes a heavy soil with plenty of nutrients. You should avoid putting it directly in the sun.

Portulacaria afra is yet another leaf succulent from Africa. It's a very tolerant plant, and will happily grow in most well-lit parts of a room. The only thing it doesn't like is too much water. If it's kept cool in winter, then (like all succulents) it should be watered much less.

This plant can achieve quite a respectable size. Its small branches grow out almost horizontally from the main stem. These in turn form smaller branches, and bear thick, round, fleshy leaves. *Portulacaria* is

particularly suited to a cactus display, because it's one of the very few succulents that is both tall and bushy in habit.

Echeverias (*Echeveria*) are a group of plants from Central America that have been popular with gardeners for centuries. In summer they can be grown in a rockery. However, many species are especially suited to the indoor environment. They need a potting mixture that is rich in nutrients. In winter you should put them in a cool, well-lit position.

The **mesembryanthemums** are the most forgiving of all the succulent plants, and they also produce some of the best floral displays. The shrubby species can also be planted out in a rock garden or in a trough on a patio. They may be covered with largish flowers for months on end. They do, however, need full sunlight in order to flower.

The mesembryanthemum family also includes some

fascinating dwarf succulents such as the tiger jaws (*Faucaria*) and the incredible living stones (*Lithops*).

Living stones grow practically on top of the ground — so when you plant them, simply spread a little sand around them. They are also very easily satisfied, and need no feeding whatsoever. Be very careful when you water them. Use very little water, and never sprinkle the body of the plant. Living stones form new fleshy leaves every year; the old ones die off.

A garden in a bottle

First you need to find the right bottle or jar for your mini-garden — and it's worth letting your imagination wander. Any suitable glass container will do, from a large wine bottle to a demijohn and from a preserving jar to a Winchester. Just make absolutely sure that the glass is completely transparent. You should also make sure it's absolutely clean, with no trace of anything that it used to contain.

If the neck of the bottle is too narrow for your hand to pass through it, you'll need some other way to get inside. It's quite easy to improvise a few tools. For example, you can fix a spoon or a fork to a stick, or to a piece of strong wire or piping. This produces a ready-made spade or rake for your mini-garden. You can use a stick with a loop of wire to insert the plants. A cork on the end of a sharp stick is ideal for pressing the soil down around the roots. A razor blade attached to a stick will come in handy for pruning or removing dead leaves. Finally, if you want to clean up the glass after putting in the soil, use a small sponge attached to the end of a stick.

Now that you've got your tools, you can start filling the container. First take a small funnel, or a rolled-up piece of cardboard or foil, and use it to feed small pieces of charcoal into the bottom of the jar. A

layer 2 inches (5 cm) deep will allow the soil to drain, and prevent a build-up of salts and algae. Now add the soil with the same funnel — use a finely divided humus mixed with about half the quantity of sand. This time you'll want a depth of about 4 inches (10 cm).

Put in the larger plants first. Arrange them either in the

A luxuriant window display.

82

middle of the jar or on the side that will be facing the wall. Your choice will depend on where in the room the jar is going to be displayed, and whether it can be seen from all sides. Put each plant in a depression in the soil, then press the soil in around the roots. You could even add a few tiny stones to create a miniature landscape.

You can even create a water garden in a jar, though you must obviously take care to control the growth of algae.

After planting you'll need to add water to the soil — but as long as the jar is kept closed, that's probably the last time you'll need to water it. From now on this miniature eco-system should be able to look after itself. The moisture that evaporates from the leaves condenses on the inside of the jar, then runs down into the soil and is absorbed by the roots. This makes a mini-garden ideal for centrally heated rooms.

However, do make sure that dead leaves are removed quickly, along with any weeds that start to grow in the soil — and if any of your plants grow too large for the bottle, you should either prune them or replace them with new ones.

There is a wide range of plants suitable for mini-gardens, among them earth stars (*Cryptanthus*) and similar bromeliads, ivy species, spider plant, prayer plant, miniature ferns, begonia species, snake plant, creeping fig, artillery plant (*Pilea*), nerve plant (*Fittonia*), string of beads (*Senecio rowleyanus*) and many others. The important thing is to buy plants that don't grow too fast.

83

An indoor water garden

Plants are often associated with particular animals — in a fish tank, for instance. If you're planning this kind of environment, you'll need to choose plants that would be found in the animals' natural habitat. However, you don't actually need fish in your fish tank. If you simply like water plants for their own sake, then a fish tank provides the ideal setting for a small water garden in your own living room. You can enjoy the sight of reflected sunlight sparkling among the greenery — and that's not all. A water garden can even improve the atmosphere of the room itself, by humidifying dry, centrally heated air.

You can start with a glass tank — choose any shape you like. First fill the bottom of the tank with a suitable plant compost. Make a few hillocks in the soil to create a kind of miniature river margin. (Later this will provide the ideal site for moisture-loving, compact plants such as the *Selaginella* (club moss).) Next lay an inch or so of sand over the top of the soil. Then add an appropriate amount of lukewarm water, and wait patiently until the potting mixture has settled down again. Now, at last, you can start planting.

The water hyacinth (*Eichhornia crassipes*), which flowers from July to September,

is well worth including in your plans, and it will not be difficult to manage.

It's best if the tank is in a well-lit position. If it isn't, you'll need to provide some additional lighting. Ordinary aquarium lights will do the job very well. However, a few carefully arranged spotlights may create a more decorative effect, turning your water garden into a really exotic display.

Water gardens don't need very much looking after. Just top up the water level to compensate for evaporation, and make sure that you remove any dead plant material.

When you feed your water garden, never use a fertiliser that contains any chloride. The best solution is to buy an NPK granule fertiliser (not powder) such as Growmore.

A water tank like this is ideal for any plants that need a lot of humidity and like to stand close together.

Growing epiphytes on a branch

Epiphytes are plants that grow on the trunks or branches of trees without actually feeding on their hosts. This makes them quite different from parasitic plants such as the mistletoe, which grows on our native trees.

Epiphytic plants can grow on any piece of wood — anything from a length of bark, a twig or a root up to a thick branch. The larger the branch, the more convincing it will look as an imitation of these plants' natural forest habitat. Pear and apple branches make excellent hosts for an epiphyte display.

When planning and arranging your display, try to create a pleasing harmony between the host branch and the epiphytes on it. Tiny plants will look rather skimpy on a thick branch. Large epiphytes will soon grow too heavy for a thin one. If you decide to create a large display, always remember that epiphytes on a branch are more difficult to water without making a mess. If you attach the branch to a piece of furniture, the dripping water will soon start to mark the veneer.

A better solution is to put the branch in a large wooden tub. The best way to anchor it is quite simply to cement it in. Get someone else to centralise and hold the branch while you infill with concrete to about half the depth of the container, allowing ample space for adding compost later. Plant some ground-cover plants such as ivy or mind your own business (*Soleirolia*) so the dead branch emerges from a living green carpet.

There are various ways of planting the epiphytes on the branch. The first method is only feasible if you keep the air warm and humid all the time

Given their origins, bromeliads are the ideal plants for an epiphyte branch.

This branch has been planted with an orchid, a bromeliad and a creeping fig to create an attractive display.

and water the plants frequently. Carefully remove each plant from its pot, then wrap the roots in sphagnum moss and secure the whole bundle with plastic-covered wire. Give the plant plenty of water and attach it to the branch, either where it forks or in a spot that you've hollowed out specifically for this purpose. A simpler method is to leave each plant in its pot and attach the pot to the branch.

When you're looking after epiphytes, be sure that you always give them enough water. Soil, moss and roots alike will need regular and generous doses of lukewarm water. If the leaves of your bromeliad form water-tight 'urns' you should keep these filled with water. From time to time you'll need to thin out the plants a little. Cut back any excess shoots from creeping or climbing plants.

A few plants such as tillandsias can be grown individually on small pieces of wood. You should plunge them into warm water about once a week, together with the moss and the wood they're attached to. Keep them underwater until the moss is fully saturated. As the water evaporates, it will create the humidity so vital to the plant's development. Give tillandsias a regular spraying too.

When you're choosing plants for an epiphyte branch, always make your initial selection from plants of one particular kind. This in itself will allow for plenty of variety.

If you start with **bromeliads**, for example, you could use any or all of the following: urn plant (*Aechmea*), *Billbergia*, *Neoregelia*, flaming sword (*Vriesea*), and tillandsia. You could then add various suitable non-bromeliads such as devil's ivy, philodendrons or *Ceropegia*.

Another alternative is to use **orchids** as the basis for your display. Most greenhouse orchids grow as epiphytes in the forest canopies where they originally come from. Your choice of orchid might well include *Cattleya*, *Cymbidium*, *Phalaenopsis* (moth orchid) and *Dendrobium* species. In the wild, it's virtually impossible to prise the roots of epiphytic orchids away from the bark of their hosts.

There's even a group of **cacti** that can be used as part of an epiphyte display. The various *Rhipsalis* species grow naturally on trees or even perched on moss-covered rocks.

Among the numerous epiphytic **ferns**, perhaps the most suitable are stag's horn fern, bird's nest fern, polypody and the various dwarf species.

A green partition

Plants aren't just pleasant to look at; they can also greatly improve the climate inside your home. They restore humidity to a dry, centrally heated atmosphere. They act as a filter for dust, which settles on the leaves and can then be washed off. Moreover, they produce oxygen during the day, though admittedly only in small amounts. You can cover a whole wall with vegetation by arranging various bushy trees with attractive leaves at the foot of the wall and then fixing hanging baskets above them.

An even more interesting possibility is a 'green partition' across the middle of a room — a partition consisting for the most part of plants. Most of these would have to be climbers or plants that grow in a tall, columnar habit. Plants that grow outwards, such as the screw-pine (*Pandanus*), would spoil the effect.

Before embarking on a green partition, start by checking the amount of available light. If there isn't enough sunlight, an extra halogen lamp on the ceiling immediately above might help to make up for it. If the partition includes a shelf, then the shade from this must also be taken into account. The best solution might be to choose shade-loving plants.

Plants on **moss sticks** can grow to great heights without taking up much space, but most of them need plenty of humidity. That means a lot of spraying, so you should choose furniture that won't be damaged as a result. Plants that are recommended for moss sticks include *Epipremnum, Philodendron,*

Schefflera, and *Cissus.* All of them dislike sun or sudden temperature changes. On the other hand they are easy to care for if they are kept humid and moderately warm.

Climbing plants are mostly grown for their attractive foliage. They don't produce very good flowers indoors, but they will give your room a very natural feel. If you want a partition made up of climbers and moss sticks, your first requirement will be a plant trough. The size of this trough will depend on how much space you have.

Now anchor a climbing frame firmly inside the trough. You can make it out of vertical and horizontal poles tied together. You could also use unusually shaped branches as a support

Above *Ferns really like the shade, making them the ideal plants for a green partition. Remember, though, that you'll need to give them plenty of humidity.*

Left *A window-sill that's out of the sun can carry a large amount of greenery — and even lets you dispense with curtains!*

for climbers. If the partition is already thick with greenery, then you can run dark-green wire across it to provide support. Tie the trailing shoots to it with raffia above each leaf node.

Climbers suitable for a partition include ivy (*Hedera*), *Epipremnum*, *Cissus*, jasmine, *Dipladenia*, and *Philodendron*. Keep them fairly moist, and feed them with fertiliser every now and then.

Putting plants outside in summer

Once a garden patio was no more than a paved area adjoining the house. It was sometimes surrounded by a balustrade, and was usually raised above the level of the garden. Steps linked it to the garden, and the adjoining slopes were often occupied by flower beds or some kind of rock garden.

Today, patios are far more versatile. When they're next to a house, they may be flush with the garden. A block of flats may have a communal patio, and some patios are effectively a kind of roof garden. The main thing they have in common is that they're paved, usually with concrete or flagstones.

This makes patios an ideal place to keep houseplants outside in the summer. If you plant them in pots, tubs or troughs, you can move them around to get them into or out of the sun — or, if you wish, you can arrange them in groups. A patio has a climate all of its own. It is usually more sheltered than the garden itself, and is also freer of draughts than a balcony.

Many houseplants really like the open air during the summer, and it also helps them to build up their strength for the winter months.

The patio is the place for all those plants that need plenty of fresh air during the summer to build up their strength for the winter. The list is endless, but would, for example, include hibiscus, chrysanthemums and most palms as well as cacti and other succulents.

Patios are usually built on the sunny side of a house. Some people like to add trellises and espaliers to support climbing plants and provide additional shelter from the wind. If the patio is really sheltered, you can often use it to put out plants that would normally prefer a warmer climate. Agaves, oleanders, plumbagos, pomegranates and thorn-apples will all flourish here, and they'll flower profusely — even in our climate — as long as you look after them properly. These plants like plenty of sunshine, but they'll also need plenty of watering and feeding. During the main growth period (May–August) you should give all your plants a regular fortnightly feed. In this case it doesn't actually matter whether you use a liquid or a powdered fertiliser.

There's one very important rule for any plant that's going to spend the winter back inside the house: stop fertilising it at the end of August. This gives the existing shoots time to harden up, so the plant will start the winter without any of those soft, young shoots that are so vulnerable to pests and disease.

During the winter you'll need to find somewhere suitable for all the so-called tub plants, including angel's trumpet, oleander, heliotrope, *Lantana*, fuchsia, hibiscus and others. They'll need a well-lit position that's frost-free and protected from draughts. You should keep them cool and water them only very sparingly; a little water every three weeks will be enough to stop them drying out. Too much watering in a cool place and the roots will rot. Too much warmth and they'll start to produce shoots, which will remain weak because there isn't enough light for them.

A display of houseplants and tub plants can turn a patio into a veritable oasis of blooms. Among the most suitable plants for this are oleander, myrtle, agave, palms, palm lily (*Yucca*), African lily, flowering maple and plumbago. Their lush greenery and brightly coloured flowers will transform your patio into an irresistible summer retreat.

Typical patio plants will merge beautifully with pots and troughs sown with plain summer annuals such as veronicas, petunias, marigolds and nasturtiums. Other, more traditional plants might include pelargoniums, begonias, fuchsias, sages, dahlias and various small shrubs. A patio can also easily accommodate one or two herbs from the vegetable garden, and maybe a tomato plant too.

Any surrounding trellises, espaliers or doorways will provide further scope for growing various woody

Houseplants will add further variety to your patio and garden displays.

climbers such as Virginia creeper, clematis, winter jasmine and honeysuckle. You could also include some of the annual climbers like sweet pea.

So a patio is far more than a summer home for sun-hungry houseplants. It can also accommodate a whole plethora of indigenous plants. There's nowhere inside the house that can offer the scope to combine so many different plants in a single, harmonious display.

January

A few plants — azaleas, for instance — will come into flower this month. They'll need plenty of water, and you should even feed them with some lime-free fertiliser. Take great care when airing the house. A sudden blast of cold air from the window is lethal for any · houseplant. Avoid placing any plants close to window panes during cold weather.

February

In winter it's particularly important to keep the air around your plants very humid. Central heating can easily damage them by making the air extremely dry. Spray your plants every day. This is also the time when they're most vulnerable to pests, so keep a close eye on the undersides of the leaves. Keep cacti in a cool, well-lit position. Don't just forget about them, though: even cacti can do with just a little watering at this stage if they're growing in very small pots.

March

Turn your attention to all the patio plants that have been overwintering in a cool room. Repot them in a moist potting mixture, put them in a warm, well-lit room, and water them frequently. That way they'll be growing vigorously by mid-May, when you put them back into the garden. On sunny days give your houseplants a good wash to remove all the dust and dirt.

These cyclamens (Cyclamen persicum) are nearing the end of their flowering period, so you should start watering them less.

April

There's still plenty of time to repot most of your houseplants. If bushier plants (e.g. papyrus, aspidistra, ornamental asparagus) have become rather large, you can divide them at this stage. Wash your plant pots thoroughly before reusing them. On mild days you could put a few plants outside to 'air', but keep them protected from direct sunlight.

May

Now's the time to start propagating your houseplants so they can develop during the main growing season. Plant out the cuttings and keep them warm. This is also the best time for transferring plants to a hydroponic medium: use pure water at first, and don't add any nutrient solution for the first ten days. You can sow your cacti now, and by the end of the month you can begin grafting. Water balcony plants regularly.

Summer is the time for repotting all those houseplants that have grown too large.

June

Put your foliage plants out in the warm rain as often as you can. Don't forget to give your indoor plants a regular weekly feed. Remove all the spent flowers to encourage new blooms and prevent seeding, which drains the plants of energy.

July

You can propagate plants from cuttings throughout the summer season. Home-grown plants always make good presents — they have that special, personal touch. Give all your plants plenty of water now. Prune some of your plants to make them bushy (e.g. myrtle, scented geranium, flowering maple, *Dipladenia* and jasmine).

Be sure to feed your plants well: yellowing leaves and stunted growth are usually a sure sign that this job has been neglected. Keep an eye out for pests, too. If removing them isn't enough to get rid of them, try a soap solution before you resort to a chemical remedy.

August

You need to protect all your houseplants from intense sunlight. The best way of doing this is to move them a bit further into the room. Roller blinds or Venetian blinds can also come in very useful here. Where root balls have become dried out, plunge them in water until they're completely saturated.

If the body of the plant is stained red (especially in cacti) it's usually a sign that even these sun-loving plants have been exposed to the full sun too quickly.

September

As soon as the nights start to become cooler, you should take your houseplants indoors overnight — although you can still leave them outside during the daytime. Keep tying up all climbing plants such as passion flowers, jasmine, wax plants, *Dipladenia* etc.

When you go on holiday, don't worry about leaving a few of your plants outside in the open air, where they will benefit from the occasional rain shower.

October

Stop fertilising all your houseplants apart from those that are still in flower. Start to give them less water, too. This is particularly important with the woody plants that you leave outside during the day to harden them up for the winter. Remember the one simple rule: the cooler the temperature, the less water you should give your plants. Don't take any more cuttings from now on — rooting is very difficult at this time of year.

November

As the days draw in, most houseplants will enter their dormant phase. If any of them have been outside during October, give them a good wash before moving them indoors. As you turn up the heating indoors, your houseplants will need more care and attention. Give them a daily spraying at the very least. Now's the time to bed down your hyacinth bulbs. Move your cacti into a cool, well-lit position for over-wintering at a temperature of about 50°F (10°C).

When the central heating is full on, you should spray most of your houseplants with lukewarm water every day.

December

When the temperatures drop, reduce watering to a minimum. The only exceptions to this are the winter-flowering cyclamens, camellias etc, which still need plenty of feeding and watering. Some foliage plants need a regular weekly spraying with lukewarm water; these include *Dieffenbachia*, *Epipremnum*, *Philodendron* and the palms. With the rubber plant and Swiss cheese plant, all you have to do is wipe their leaves with a wet sponge. Give the cacti an airing every now and then, and use water on them very sparingly. When airing your plants, be sure to protect them from draughts.

Index